Child language, learning and linguistics

15/11

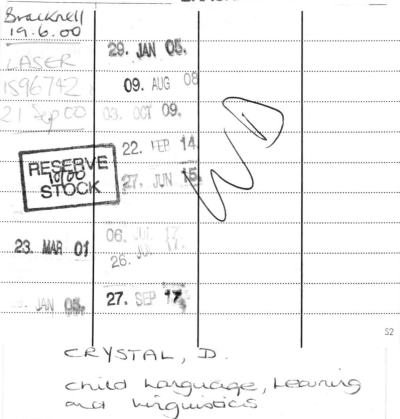
CRYSTAL, D.
Child Language, Learning
and Linguistics

CLASS NO. 401.9

0713 158 905 0 916 6B

Child language, learning and linguistics

An overview for the teaching and therapeutic professions

David Crystal

Professor of Linguistic Science, University of Reading

Edward Arnold

First published 1976 by
Edward Arnold (Publishers) Ltd
25 Hill Street, London W1X 8LL

ISBN cloth: 0 7131 5890 5 ✓
     paper: 0 7131 5891 3

Printed in Great Britain by
Billing & Sons Limited,
Guildford, London and Worcester

Contents

Preface

This book is primarily an expansion of a series of lectures developed for in-service courses to teachers, speech therapists and others, mainly between 1973 and 1976. It also contains revised sections of material that has appeared in article form. Parts of chapter 3 are taken from 'Neglected linguistic principles in the study of reading' in D. Moyle (ed.), *Reading: what of the future?* (Proceedings of the United Kingdom Association, 1974; London, Ward and Lock Educational Books 1975); 'Linguistic perspectives' in the special number of *Reading* on the Bullock Report (June 1975), vol. 9, pp. 37–49; and 'The educational use of linguistics' (The Coloma College Conference, July 1973; Department of Education and Science), pp. 1–9, reprinted in *ERIC Reports* (Jan. 1973, No. ED 091 939). Earlier versions of parts of chapters 1 and 2 were recorded on cassette as part of the short talks series of the University of Reading's Centre for the Teaching of Reading.

I am extremely grateful to several colleagues for their comments on early drafts of this book: Paul Fletcher, Michael Garman, Arthur Hughes, Paul Mercier, Hilary Norman, John Trim, Peter Trudgill, Renata Whurr and Roberta Wilkins; also to Sarah Mozley, for her editorial advice and assistance. And an anonymous vote of thanks must go to the several speech therapists and teachers who have allowed me to participate in their classes and clinics, and who have helped shape my theoretical views in the light of their experiences.

David Crystal

March 1976

Introduction

There are two main ways to present the subject of linguistics, the scientific study of language. One is to see it as an end in itself, an academic study in its own right, followed because of the challenge to understand one of the most fascinating and complex facets of human behaviour. The other is to see it as a 'service discipline', as a science which can be of value to the community as a whole, and of specific assistance to certain professions within it. I have on various occasions approached the subject of linguistics from the first point of view;[1] the present volume proposes to explore it from the second, bearing in mind the needs of a range of professional interests that have been relatively neglected in recent years. The area of primary relevance with which I am concerned is the learning of language, whether normal or abnormal, by children, and its study by the main professions of nursery and primary school teaching, the various branches of special education, educational psychology, speech therapy and the teaching of the deaf. Closely related fields, such as nursing, health visiting, social care, and paediatrics are not to be ignored, for language is a pervasive phenomenon, which needs a combined attack on many fronts if the problems it provides the learner are to be solved; and all these areas have a contribution to make. Above all, the definition of what a professional awareness of language involves must be related, at every point, to the needs and feelings of the parents, often left on the sidelines of a debate amongst professionals as to the needs and future of their child, especially when language handicap is involved. By focusing on the common basis implicit in the linguistic interests of the various professions, and by grounding the study of child language in the home and local community, I hope that a better-founded understanding and cooperation will emerge that will benefit the learning child. I am aware that I am stating the obvious to many who represent these professions. But for a book with 'linguistics' in its title, the point needs to be made at the beginning, so that my position will be clear.

When I say that a common basis for language study is implicit in

[1] *Linguistics* (Harmondsworth, Penguin 1971); *What is linguistics?* (3rd edition, London, Edward Arnold 1974).

the various professions mentioned above, I choose my words carefully. This aspect of 'applied linguistics' has been one of the least studied, compared with the intensive and long-standing work that has gone on under this heading in relation to foreign-language teaching.[2] Language is certainly a common concern, in theory, but in practice the way in which it has been studied has often been divisive, each profession having its own traditions, methods, priorities and pride, and often not communicating with others, or aware of the strength of areas of expertise other than its own. All this is understandable, and there is no argument here for the development of a 'super-therapist' who can handle all aspects of language development and disability equally efficiently. This is probably not possible, language being so complex, and is probably not desirable, when one sees the success of the 'team' approach to the analysis and remediation of language and its troubles. But there is an argument here for the development of a common basis of understanding that is *explicit*, so that the specific expertises of the various professions relating to language can be clearly defined and interrelated, and thus unnecessary overlap, duplication of effort and conflict, in both research and teaching, avoided. For overlap and duplication there is. It is not difficult to point to research being reported in the journal of one profession that is essentially the same as that reported in another. And there is conflict too, more often unconscious than conscious, as one can often observe between the language policies of remedial and general teacher, speech therapist and teacher of the deaf, or primary and junior school. The argument of this book is that by making everyone's feelings, assumptions and methods about language explicit, such problems can be at least anticipated, and possibly resolved. But explicitness, coherence and general perspective can be achieved only by a systematic study of the nature and use of language, and that is linguistics.

This argument will not be an easy one to make convincing, because of the ambiguous standing of linguistics in the eyes of the public at large. For a variety of reasons discussed in later chapters, linguistics is felt to be 'relevant' to all of the professions concerned with the assessment, development and remediation of language. I know this to be so, because I have been invited to lecture about linguistics on many occasions to groups from all of the above professions. In fact this book is basically a systematization and expansion of these lectures. But going far beyond this in their influence are the references to linguistics made by the many in-service courses, discussion groups and publications of various kinds which have emerged particularly since 1970. Linguistics also figures prominently in the recommendations of the two major

---

[2] See, for example, D. A. Wilkins, *Linguistics in language teaching* (Edward Arnold 1972).

government reports which have appeared in recent years.[3] To take two examples, the College of Speech Therapists has since 1974 formally recognized linguistics as part of its syllabus, and Recommendation 133 of the Bullock Report states that 'Linguistics and other specialist studies of language have a considerable contribution to make to the teaching of English".It is therefore not surprising that there are feelings of 'relevance' around. But, as suggested above, the situation is not entirely clear. Sometimes these feelings are based on evidence, for example of a real and productive collaboration between linguist and teacher (as with the reading project, *Breakthrough to Literacy*). But more often they are based on a vaguely held principle—that there *ought* to be a connection, perhaps because linguistics is a 'science', and a scientific approach to something is generally held to be for the good. Especially in the remedial professions, where the need for systematic guidelines for the understanding and treatment of disorders is as urgent now as it ever was, the favourable connotations of a 'scientific' approach have commended themselves. As the Bullock recommendation implies, a great deal of thought has been given to the prospect of seeing language learning in a linguistic perspective, and as a result many people in the professions, especially those who have been in the field a long time, or who have missed out on the newer courses of training, feel out of date and even threatened, especially when confronted by someone who *has* mastered some terminology, and who feels the need to hide lack of experience by an over-use of it! It has been a repeated experience to have my lectures on linguistics introduced to audiences of teachers and others by a 'chairperson' who admits to being 'scared' of linguistics. The chairperson and audience are presumably prepared to believe there must be something in the subject (for otherwise why would they have come?), but have evidently been upset by its appearance in textbooks, or perhaps, by its presentation by the subject's practitioners.

I sympathize. It is indeed the case that linguistics is not as yet a particularly accessible subject, despite the range of introductory textbooks written in recent years. All of these, including my own, are of limited value to the above professions, because they lack the desired orientation to classroom or clinical problems, and they presuppose a certain amount of background. To expect professional colleagues outside of the environment of higher education to attack the voluminous and technical literature on linguistics presupposes a considerable degree of motivation, and (perhaps more important) leave of absence or time—a combination of circumstances that is understandably rare in these days of budgetary cuts and shortage of staff. For the majority it is the *initial*

---

[3] *Speech therapy services* (London, HMSO 1972—the 'Quirk Report'); *A language for life* (HMSO 1975—the 'Bullock Report').

motivation to study linguistics which is lacking—and where can this come from? Reading the linguistics literature will not usually help, for as already remarked, this is often off-putting—and to argue this in any case begs the question. To begin reading a textbook presupposes motivation. Moreover, these books, usually oriented towards the state of mind of students, and attempting to present the *basis* of the discipline of linguistics, do not usually concern themselves much with attempting to make a bridge between their content and the language professions. But this is precisely what is needed, so that an unmotivated reader can see in advance what the point of the exercise is. 'Is it worth getting involved?' is the real question, and the only convincing answer is: 'Because it helps. Because, if one does, one's professional role—at least, as regards language—will in some way become more comprehensible, more principled, more productive.' If people can be persuaded at the outset that this is likely, it may well provide them with the motivation to go further with linguistics, and master those aspects of the complexity of language science which are the means to this end. For let there be no misunderstanding: there *has to be* complexity. Language is complex. Language disturbance, in its myriad forms, is highly complex. There can be no simple, short solution to the problems posed by language. To expect that there will be is to live in an unreal world (which I shall discuss further in chapter 3). Linguistics at any rate offers no panacea. But what this subject can do is provide a basis, a framework, a set of guidelines which can be used in both an analytic and a remedial way by those professionally involved. This inevitably makes demands on time and intellect. The argument of this book is that it is worth it.

What then is the basis of this argument? It is essentially threefold. First, while everything in linguistics, viewed as a science of language, could be relevant to the professional analysis of language behaviour, by no means the whole of the subject needs to be encountered or understood in order to arrive at the linguistic perspective outlined above. Any aspect of the subject *could* throw light on practical problems. But which aspects do, at present, and which do not? It is not so obvious how one should draw the line between relevant and irrelevant. And here there is no substitute for the linguist to have spent hundreds of hours of observation and participation in class or clinic, in order to learn enough of the priorities, methods and terminology of the various professions so as to develop his sense of 'relevance'. Not even regular collaborative discussions with teaching or therapist colleagues can replace this. My view of which ideas are basic and most relevant in linguistics will therefore be the subject-matter of chapter 1.

Secondly, one has to be aware of the hypotheses about learning, education, community health, and so on that relate to language. It is not the business of the linguist to define these, of course; rather, his aim is to make clear exactly what is involved in them, and in particular to assess the practicality and coherence of proposals relating to language learning and use in children. One of the theses of this book is that many fine arguments have been presented concerning improving language abilities in class or elsewhere, but that insufficient thought has been given as to how these proposals should be implemented—or whether they *can* be, in the present state of our knowledge of language. These arguments and hypotheses, then, I take from the recent literature on language and education, and especially the positions advocated by the government reports mentioned above, which have set the educational linguistic tone of the 1970s.

Thirdly, one has to be aware of the crucial interpenetration of the study of child language with that of the adult language, and in particular, the language used by the individual teacher or therapist. This should be evident if we consider the two main areas of involvement on the part of the language professions. (a) We are concerned to determine how language development in normal children can be made to fulfil their full potential in school and pre-school, not only in their comprehension and use of spoken English but also in reading and writing, and in the use of these modalities across the curriculum. A quotation from Bullock seems appropriate:

> all genuine learning involves discovery . . . to exploit the process of discovery through language in all its uses is the surest means of enabling a child to master his mother tongue. (§4.10)

(b) For children presenting some degree of language handicap, the concern is to determine how best their abnormal language development can be identified, assessed and remedied. A quotation from Quirk seems appropriate:

> the would-be practitioner of therapy, whether of speech, of hearing, of reading or of writing, must in future regard *language* as the central core of his basic discipline . . . (§6.60) more attention should be given to speech and language in longitudinal studies of child development. (§10.13)

In both areas, I shall argue, these aims can best be fulfilled by beginning with an understanding of the adult language—and thus with linguistics, which is where most study of the adult language has taken place. This apparently back-to-front argument—we begin to study child language by studying adult language—has a ready justification. Both areas need some kind of yardstick so that progress in language development, or lack of it, can be assessed. The desirable measure here—and indeed the only practicable measure at present—is that provided by normal child language studies (see chapter 2). We establish the normal pattern of development, as far as possible, and then use this as an index of comparison. But the notion of 'adult language' now intervenes, of necessity, in two ways. Firstly, adult language is the goal of the whole exercise. Unless we are aware, in detail, of the nature of the behaviour we are expecting children to acquire, it will be difficult to lead children towards it in a principled way. Secondly, adult language is a necessary component of any assessment process. Until such time as children can assess themselves, the adults involved in the interaction need to be aware of their own language, how they are using it, whether it is too simple or too difficult or simply inappropriate. Without this awareness, it is impossible to avoid the charge that is is *they* and not the child who is at fault, when remedial language work fails to produce any effect. 'Know thyself' is a relevant maxim in all child language studies. And it is this which leads us to linguistics, which in the past 50 years has concerned itself very largely with the study of the adult language—how best to describe it, analyse it, explain it. And that is why the book starts here.

All of this inevitably plays down the nonlinguistic aspects of the field—the psychological, biological, educational and other accounts of child development. There is little in this book about the audiological, psychological, neurological and other preconditions for language development and use. This exclusion is the main constraint on the book's construction. My intention is to focus on a particular area of neglect, the linguistic study of language, which for the sake of argument I am treating as central. I will then move from this centre to consider the points of contact between a linguistic view of things and those of other disciplines, especially teaching (where most of the published discussion has taken place). This can hardly be systematic, in the present state of the art, but I hope it will be illuminating, and define more clearly what is the potential contribution of a linguist to any team involved in the complex processes of language teaching, assessment and remediation.

Chapter I   Linguistics

Linguistics, the scientific study of language, has had a very recent and rapid development in this country. In the early 1960s only two or three universities gave it any formal recognition as an academic subject; but nowadays it is taught and researched throughout the higher education sector. Many universities now run a BA course in linguistics, or in linguistics combined with some other subject, such as English, psychology, or a modern language. What are the reasons for this rapid development?

It is fairly clear, in looking back, that the 1960s brought an increased awareness of the importance and complexity of language as a form of human behaviour. This was most noticeable in the various 'applied' fields of language study (such as foreign-language teaching, translation, speech pathology, mother-tongue teaching) where a real demand grew up to get to grips with the facts of language structure and use. How can we teach a foreign language without being fully aware of the structural differences between the foreign language and the mother tongue? How can we guide a speech-disordered child towards normal usage without a clear understanding both of the structural characteristics of the disorder *and* of normal usage? How can we develop the communicative abilities of the young child if we do not understand the range of communicative expression encountered in the language as a whole, and the stage which his own language development has already reached? Such questions paralleled those being asked in many research areas too: philosophers, psychologists, anthropologists and others were finding that many of the problems they had to deal with were intimately bound up with the study of language. In particular, the whole question of the role of language in relation to the human mind was reopened; and it was the personal impact in this area of Noam Chomsky, Professor of Linguistics at the Massachusetts Institute of Technology, that brought the greatest publicity for the broader implications of the scientific study of language.

Our awareness of the importance of language may have increased in the 1960s, but of course language-awareness as such is nothing new. People have been studying language as long as there have been records of their studying anything. Plato and Aristotle both wrote at length about language, for example. Why then was a linguistics necessary?

Why could we not have continued with our traditional information about language, accumulated over several hundred years? There are both negative and positive answers to be given to this question, and they are bound up with a consideration of the definition given above. linguistics as the *science* of language. The negative reason is that our traditional store of linguistic knowledge simply did not satisfy the demands for hard facts and relevant theories made by the new language investigators of the 1960s. The positive reason is that the scientific approach on the face of it *did* seem able to provide the kind of information of value to teacher, therapist, and the like. So let us look at both these reasons in greater detail.

This is no place for a general discussion about science, but it is helpful to begin by considering some of the characteristics generally associated with a scientific approach. Four stand out: it should be systematic, comprehensive, precise and objective. To say that there is now a science of language is to suggest that previous language work was in some sense *not* scientific—that is, *lacking* in system, comprehensiveness, precision and objectivity—and that this was a bad thing. On the whole this was so. The weaknesses of the traditional approaches to language study in these respects are well recognized, and discussed in any introduction to linguistics; so I will not dwell on them here. But it is worth remembering that many of the difficulties encountered in studying language have arisen directly out of the inadequacies of the earlier approaches. For instance, traditional grammars dealt with a very restricted amount of language. On the whole they concentrated on describing the written language, providing very little information about the forms of speech, which are often markedly different (see further below). There were restrictions on the style of language dealt with, too: plenty of description and illustration of the more formal and literary styles of English; next to none of the informal, colloquial styles. Thus we find rules of usage formulated and applied to the language as a whole, whereas in fact they are appropriate for the formal styles only. A good example of the confusion which arises is in the rule that sentences should not end with a preposition in English—that 'This is the man I was talking to' ought to be 'This is the man to whom I was talking.' The artificiality of this proscription is immediately apparent; but it takes systematic surveys of usage to establish the facts of the matter— in this case, that putting the preposition at the end is a perfectly normal construction in the more *informal* varieties of educated speech. If traditional grammars had presented such facts about stylistic variation, a great deal of subsequent pedagogical confusion might have been avoided.

If we are not systematic in language study, of course, then we are bound to end up with an oversimplified and impressionistic picture of the language. Moreover we run the risk of leaving things out—and this has also happened. One of the most important areas of pronunciation study was regularly ignored until the advent of modern linguistics: this was the area of intonation, rhythm, stress, and the range of effects generally referred to as 'tone of voice'. Their importance for the foreign learner, or for the child wishing to develop expressiveness in language use, is obvious; but until recently there was not even a remotely accurate description of the complex facts of intonation in English.[1]

And many other areas of language study received comparably little treatment in traditional approaches. In grammar, for instance, there was a great deal of selectivity and impressionism. For example, we are told much about the defective and irregular verbs in a language, but relatively little about the problems of describing the others—the normal, regular verbs. Or again, most of us will remember a problem over where in a sentence to put the adverb *only*. Must it go next to the word it modifies (as in *I saw only John*), or may it be separated from it (as in *I only saw John*)? Much space was spent on this question; but what about all the other adverbs in the language? Where do *they* go? What are the rules? There is considerable flexibility for some adverbs, but not for others. In the following examples, the differences appear to be mainly matters of emphasis. *Quickly John ran home. John quickly ran home. John ran quickly home. John ran home quickly.* But if we take an adverb such as *happily*, then the difference between initial and end placement is no longer one of emphasis: *Happily John came home. John came home happily.* The first means 'Thank goodness John came home', whereas the second means 'John came home in a happy state.' There are many such variations of this kind. Where do we find an analysis or classification of all the possibilities? Certainly not in any traditional textbook. Indeed, it is only recently that linguists have got around to giving such areas of grammar the attention they deserve. The first reference grammar of modern English to pay attention to such points, and to the facts of informal speech, appeared as recently as 1972.[2]

We must also not forget that one of the reasons why traditional accounts of language were of little value to modern investigators was that they were vague in several crucial respects. No language study can do without technical terms of some kind, and it is up to the investigator to ensure that whatever terms he uses are clearly defined, and used consistently. I am not thinking here of the imposing creations of some

[1] See the discussion in D. Crystal, *The English tone of voice: essays in intonation, prosody and paralanguage* (Edward Arnold 1975).
[2] R. Quirk, S. Greenbaum, G. Leech and J. Svartvik, *A grammar of contemporary English* (1972); an abridged version by Quirk and Greenbaum appeared in 1973, *A university grammar of English*; a shorter and restructured account, aimed primarily at foreign-language teaching, appeared in 1975, by Leech and Svartvik, *A communicative grammar of English*. All these books are published in London by Longman.

modern linguists, but of the traditional terminology, whose technicality we often forget because it is so familiar—terms like *word, sentence, noun, plural*. It is so easy to give these terms different senses. What is a noun, for example? Is a noun simply a 'common' noun, such as *table* and *chair*, or do we include the so-called 'proper nouns', like *John* and *London*? Are words like *rich* and *poor* (as in 'the poor are hungry') best called nouns? Or words which seem to be a cross between nouns and pronouns, such as *someone* and *everyone*, or between nouns and verbs, such as *walking* and *fishing*? Some analysts would group all these together as types of noun; others would call some nouns, and others as separate parts of speech. The point is that terminology varies, and cannot be taken for granted in language work, no more than in any other subject. But it is particularly crucial for language scholars interested in applications to be aware of this point, as so many aspects of this work are comparative. For instance, we want to say that style A is different from style B in certain specific respects; or that child A is linguistically more advanced than child B. To make comparisons, our terms of reference must be clear. And the trouble with the traditional accounts was that central terms were often not defined, or were glossed in a highly unclear way. 'A sentence is a complete thought' provides one example.

No one would, I hope, ever want to deny the historical importance of traditional scholarship, or the stimulus which this gave to the growth of modern linguistics. But at the same time, it has to be said that the pre-twentieth-century work was of little direct applicability to the problems of the present day, for the reasons mentioned. Linguistics has tried to remedy these deficiencies, and it is this which is the basis of the positive arguments referred to above for the relevance of this subject. I would in fact summarize the contribution that linguistics has made to our understanding of language under three headings: empirical, methodological and theoretical. By an empirical contribution I mean that linguistics has accumulated information about the *facts* of language structure and use. Surveys of usage have been carried out, and investigators have been trained in the techniques of accurate transcription and analysis. There are now relatively complete manuals of pronunciation for English; there are some broadly based and detailed grammars; there are a number of comprehensive dictionaries; and the facts of the less well-studied styles (such as the scientific, and the collo-quial) have begun to be covered. (It perhaps does not need emphasizing that a great deal remains to be done.)

By a methodological contribution I mean that linguistics tries to make its methods for studying language as clear and explicit as possible. After all, in a sense there are no such things as facts: facts change depending on how we find out about them. So the ways of finding out about language themselves have to be studied. What kind of language is being analysed—that is to say, what sample of language has been chosen? To what extent will the sex, socioeconomic background, age or social role of the participants in the sample affect the kind of language they use? What kind of statistical techniques are being used to set up our norms? These questions, along with the whole matter of terminology already mentioned, have now received partial answers.

Thirdly, there is the theoretical contribution. Science is far more than a collection of facts and methods: it also attempts to interrelate the facts, to see patterns in the data, to arrive at explanations of why the facts are as they are. In language study too, we have to produce a coherent account of the data, language. Can we establish a set of explanatory principles which can account for language's structure and use? Can we construct models of language which will help us to focus and shape our understanding of these abstract principles? Can we construct a comprehensive framework within which our observations about different features of language can be organized? The necessity to do such things is another favourite theme of Chomsky's, and controversy on these points provides the nucleus of the present-day subject.

It is important for anyone encountering linguistics for the first time to balance these three contributions, as all three are essential to the scientific approach to language. But it is perhaps most useful to begin with the empirical, as it is the novel information about the *facts* of the contemporary language that for many people is the most convincing argument for doing linguistics at all. If one has not done any linguistics before, then the examples in the following pages ought to be fresh and illuminating, and suggest alternative views about language to those one may now hold. It is on this assumption that the argument of this book rests.

It is, fortunately, nowadays a truism that the spoken language is different from the written language; but one of the things that has emerged very clearly from linguistic research is that the *extent* of the difference between the two media is very much greater than was previously imagined. Many people still operate with a stereotype of spoken English, which they perhaps derive from the BBC, or from public speakers, and which is strongly influenced by the norms of the written language, by the pressures of formal occasions, and by the need to be clear and precise. Few of us have ever tried or been in a position to listen in detail to the normal linguistic variability which characterizes natural, everyday, spontaneous, informal conversation, which constitutes the vastly greater part of a person's speech. This is not very surprising, of course, as my phrase 'been in a position to' implies. It is not easy to obtain good samples of real spontaneous conversation. We cannot approach someone in the street and ask him to produce a sample of natural everyday spontaneous conversation for our taperecorder! When most people see a microphone, they instinctively alter their speech: they begin to talk more carefully, they hesitate differently, and so on. Only the experienced can learn to ignore the microphone, and these, by definition, are not typical speakers. So what should one do? Hide the microphone? In pre-Watergate days, this was a common enough procedure in linguistic research, and still is (though with the difference from Watergate that one now tells one's 'informants' afterwards what has happened, and asks their permission to use the material); but obviously such recording sessions are not easy to arrange. This is one reason why information about everyday English has been so long forthcoming. Only since the development of the taperecorder and associated techniques (in other words since the 1940s) has it been possible to 'capture' speech in this way, and it was only in the 1960s that surveys of the pronunciation, grammar and vocabulary of con-versational speech became at all comprehensive and systematic. It is accordingly not surprising that this material is only now beginning to find its way into the applied areas that form the subject-matter of this book. At long last, however, a good quantity of well-recorded material is now available, and observations made about its linguistic character. When I say, then, that people tend to operate with a stereotype of spoken English, it is to spontaneous, everyday conversation that I am referring —to that kind of language used on informal occasions, when there is no pressure to speak carefully or precisely, but people are . . . just 'talking'. It is the kind of language we associate with our home, or club, or common-room—and of course the kind of language that dominates the environment of children, before they go to school. This is why it is important to study it in detail, because any assessment of language development presupposes an accurate and realistic evaluation of the language of the home.

Textbooks are partly to blame for this stereotype. If we think for a moment of the specimens of English which we are often presented with under the heading of 'conversation' (for example, in the dialogues of foreign-language teaching textbooks) it is difficult to avoid the con-clusion that they are highly stylized—stiff imitations of the dynamic spontaneity of real life. With few exceptions, the language of tape-recorded dialogues is controlled, relatively formal, and articulated clearly by fluent professionals, either phoneticians or actors, reading from scripts. The characters which are developed in textbook families are nice, decent, and characterless; the situations in which they find themselves are generally unreal or dull. People in textbooks, it seems, are not allowed to tell long or unfunny jokes, to get irritable or to lose their temper, to gossip (especially about other people), to speak with their mouths full, to talk nonsense, or swear (even mildly). They do not get all mixed up while they are speaking, forget what they wanted to say, hesitate, make grammatical mistakes, argue erratically or vaguely, get interrupted, talk at the same time, switch speech styles, manipulate the rules of the language to suit themselves, or fail to understand. In a word, they are not *real*. Real people, as everybody knows, do all these things, and it is this which is part of the essence of informal conversation. It is not something, either, which can be readily captured in radio drama or stage drama or the dialogue of novels. These art forms inevitably impose a level of organization and coherence on language that is generally lacking in everyday chat. Some forms of drama (such as the television soap operas) can get fairly close to every-day speech at times, but still superimpose a great deal of artefact. It would be a very boring and uneventful television series if it were not so.

Here are some illustrations of the extent of the difference between speech and writing. In syntax, to begin with, there is often an unspoken assumption that whatever spoken English is, its structures will for the most part be very similar to those we are used to working with in the description of written language. But there are fundamental differences, affecting even our most central grammatical concepts. Take the notion of 'sentence', for example. In the study of written English this rarely causes any problems: a sentence is something that begins with a capital letter and ends with a mark of final punctuation (full-stop, question-mark, etc.); and this definition is satisfactory for most purposes (a few writing styles are exceptional, e.g. advertising and legal English). But in speech it is *very* often difficult to say where one sentence ends and the next begins—and the important point is that this does not seem to matter, the intelligibility of the utterance not being affected by this indecision on the grammarian's part. Here is an unpunctuated utter-ance which illustrates the problem:

> There are really three issues here the first is a matter of confidence the second is a matter of safety and the third is one of convenience.

There is no difficulty over intelligibility here, but how many sentences are there? In writing, we have to make up our mind, and punctuate it either as a single sentence, with a colon after 'here', or as a sequence of sentences, either two or three or four. (Read this utterance aloud to a group, and people will arrive at different decisions.) But in speech the whole point is that we do *not* have to make up our minds: the intonation, pause and flow of the meaning will make the utterance clear, and the decision about 'sentenceness' is strictly irrelevant. Similarly, the use of the word *and* poses special problems. Two coordinated clauses can be punctuated in one of two basic ways:

> John came at three, and Mary came at four.
> John came at three. And Mary came at four.

In writing, the choice is clear: either we view the two clauses as constituting a single sentence, or the second is seen as a kind of 'afterthought' to the first. But in speech the move from one interpretation to the other is much less clear. The normal melodic interpretation of the first version would be to put a rising pitch movement on 'three', followed by a slight pause, and a falling pitch on 'four'. If the sentence is spoken in this way, and people are asked to write it down, they will do so punctuating the utterance as a single sentence. But the more the pitch movement on 'three' is made to fall, the more people will tend to punctuate the utterance as two sentences; and likewise, if we gradually increase the length of the pause, the more we move in the direction of a two-sentence reaction. The point is that in speech, intonation and pause (and related features) provide us with continua along which we can range—as if we were able to vary the degrees of size or blackness of our punctuation marks. It is perfectly possible to say the above sentence with such an intonation and pause that no one could be sure which of the two versions we were intending; and in spontaneous conversation people do this all the time.

As a third example, consider the following transcribed conversational extract.[3] (The transcription conventions for this and subsequent extracts are as follows: the end of each intonation unit is marked with | ; pauses by . , -, - - (increasing in length); words carrying the main pitch movement are in capitals, with the accent reflecting the direction of pitch; ' indicates a stressed syllable; speech in brackets is said by the listener.)

X ... I 'had er about 'five 'thousand BOOKS| - to 'take 'back to
'senate HOUSE YESTERDAY| - and I got 'all the 'way 'through the
COLLEGE| to 'where the CAR was| at the 'parking meter at the
OTHER end| and 'realized I'd 'left my . COAT| in my LOCKER| and I
'just couldn't

Y M|

X FACE| going 'all the way BACK again| with 'this great . you know
my ARMS were 'aching|

Y M|

X and I thought WELL| I'll 'get it on TUESDAY| -

Given appropriate intonation, pauses, speed variations, and the like, this sounds perfectly fluent and appropriately casual (given the occasion,

[3] It is taken from D. Crystal and D. Davy, *Investigating English style* (Longman 1969), 98.

an evening chat over coffee). There are two questions to raise which show the problems for the sentence analyst. If writing the dialogue down, would he put a full stop after 'aching' or not? The introduction of the 'agreement-noise' in the following line makes one wonder. Miss X hardly pauses at all after the word, but continues straight on with 'and I thought'. . . . There was just time for Miss Y to insert a 'M' into the conversation. The second point to note is the loose coordination between the clauses. This is quite a typical feature of conversational English. It seems to be organized along the lines of clause + clause + clause . . ., each clause being linked using a conjunction, or by intonation. Some-times the 'sentence' seems to go on for minutes, interspersed with numerous changes of direction, partial repetitions, and the like, all of which are far more frequent in everyday conversation than we tend to realize. Here is a more extensive extract to illustrate the point.[4] It is taken from a conversation between two friends (both housewives, one a teacher, the other a nurse by profession), at a point where one is telling the other about a recent holiday.

we 'had our BRÉAKFAST| (*laughs*) in the KÍTCHEN| – and 'then we 'sort

of . 'did 'what we LÍKED| and er 'got 'ready to 'go ÓUT| (M̄) we ŬSUALLY

'went 'out 'quite 'soon 'after 'that| – erm . the 'children were 'always

ŬP| at the 'crack of DĂWN| . (M̄) with the FĂRMER| – and they 'went in

the MĪLKING 'sheds| and 'helped him 'feed the PĪGS| and 'all THĪS|

you 'know we 'didn't SĒE the 'children| – – and er 'then we 'used to 'go

ŌUT| 'we – we had 'super WĔATHER| – – 'absolutely SŬPER| – and 'so

we 'went to a BĒACH| . 'usually . for er but by a'bout 'four o'clock it

. we were 'hot and we 'had to come 'off the BĔACH| (M̄|M̄) – so we'd .

'generally 'go for a TĒA 'somewhere| 'just in 'case 'supper was DELÁYED

'you 'know| (*laughs*) *laughs* and 'then we'd 'get BÁCK| and the 'children

would 'go 'straight 'back 'on to the FÁRM| . (M̄) . and 'have PŎNIES| .

their ŏWN 'children had 'ponies| and they'd . come 'up and 'put them

on the 'ponies' BĂCKS| and er – and the 'milking it was MĪLKING 'time|

and RĔALLY| we were com'mitted to 'getting BĂCK for 'milking 'time|

(M̄) for the CHILDREN| (YĔAH| *laughs*) . and 'feeding ŪP 'time| and

'putting the GĒESE to 'bed| and 'all THÍS| and erm . 'one of the 'cats

---

[4] The extract comes from D. Crystal and D. Davy, *Advanced conversational English* (Longman 1975), 62.

'had KÍTTENS| and er 'oh you KNÓW| 'all THĪS 'sort of thing| . it 'had

them in a 'big 'box in the KÌTCHEN| in this 'box of STRÀW| – 'and erm

– – 'it was just GRÊAT|

There are various points of grammar raised by such data, over and above the question of clause coordination already mentioned. Perhaps the most important point is to emphasize that such loosely structured clause sequences only remain intelligible if certain conditions are present. In particular, there must be an appropriate intonation and rhythm, and there must be thematic structure to the discourse—a process of pausing, recapitulation and comment which permits the listener to keep up and react (note the use of the 'M's' of agreement in the above extract). It is difficult to illustrate the force of intonation in a book, but it is easy to show other aspects of the organization of the utterance. As an example, let us take the set of 'comment clauses' that this kind of conversation uses with frequency—such items as *you know, you see, mind you, I mean*, and 'fillers' like *sort of*. The use of these items in speech has often been criticized—they are said to be signs of 'sloppy' speech, of 'imprecise thinking', of 'boring' speech, and so on. But such criticisms are misplaced. It is true that over-use of these phrases can lead to speech behaviour that is irritating and incomprehensible, and it is true that there are many linguistic occasions when we may prefer the speaker to do without them (when we are expecting a precise answer in a tele- vision interview, for example). But these are not the occasions being discussed here. In informal conversation they have a proper role, as they are one of the main means language has of expressing the various alterations in the force and direction of argument that we find ourselves using. In informal situations, it is perfectly possible to start a new sentence before the old one is finished, to break the syntax by introduc- ing a clarification, to be vague or imprecise. Indeed, on such occasions, it might be argued, the opposite world would be the undesirable one—a world where every sentence emerges with impeccable balance, enshrin- ing precisely articulated thoughts in layer upon layer of neatly integrated syntactic structure. People need to relax, and the linguistic signs of their relaxation are evident in the syntactic flexibility they introduce into their conversation. The important point to note is that these linguistic markers of stylistic and semantic informality do not lack grammar. It is not up to the individual how he uses these comment clauses—how he pronounces them, where he puts them in a sentence, and so on. They are governed by rules of usage, as any other area of grammar. These rules may not much resemble the traditional gramma- tical rules of school textbooks, but rules they are none the less. And, as a corollary, it is possible to make mistakes in their use—as foreigners learning English conversation usually discover. For example, a clause like *you know* may occur at the beginning, middle or end of a clause, but its intonation varies with its position, as does its meaning. In initial position, for instance, it tends to be high in pitch and rapidly articulated, as in:

you know, I think you ought to go home.

This has a largely stylistic effect, which softens the force of what follows —a kind of vocal expression of sympathy for the listener's position. If it is not present in the above example, the following sentence immediately sounds more abrupt:

I think you ought to go home.

In middle position, the intonation and meaning are different. The pitch is lower, and usually preceded by some kind of hesitation. This expresses the fact that the speaker feels some part of what he has said to be unclear or ambiguous: the *you know* introduces a fresh attempt to get his meaning across, or to explain some aspect of his meaning further, as in:

I'm just going to the shop—you know, the one on the corner.

In final position, there are many possibilities of pronunciation; e.g. with a high pitch and a rising tone, it is a quick way of asking the listener to agree, or to confirm that what has been said has been understood, as in:

so he went over to Pete's place, you know?

With a low pitch and rising tone, and preceded by a pause, the phrase takes on a more literal force, almost like 'surely you *must* know'. It indicates that it is unnecessary for the speaker to complete his meaning, because he assumes that the listener is quite aware of the point at issue, as in:

I've just been to see Mrs Jones and—you know!

This use is often accompanied by a wink or nudge, implying that there is something about Mrs Jones that is significant or scandalous, which need not be gone into, and which perhaps *ought* not to be gone into!

These illustrate something of the range of nuances that this phrase can have. Also to be noted are the grammatical restrictions on the use of the phrase. For example, it is normal to find *you know* with statements, but very unlikely with questions ('you know, is it six o'clock?'), commands ('you know, shut the door') or exclamations ('you know, damn'). And there are similar restrictions on the use of the other phrases of this general kind. We may certainly be imprecise or change our minds in informal conversation, but it is necessary to do this grammatically.

There are many other examples of colloquial syntax that could be chosen to illustrate the point about speech/writing differentiation (e.g. the use of contracted forms, such as *isn't*), but none are so pervasive as the features which link clauses into connected speech.[5] Likewise, it would be possible to illustrate the distinctiveness of informal conversation from its vocabulary, where there are many thousands of words that tend to be avoided in the written language, and indeed, over whose spelling there is often a considerable degree of doubt, e.g. *thingummy, whatyoumaycallit*. Some of the educational implications of this I shall discuss in chapter 3. For the moment it is enough to emphasize that investigations into the nature of speech data of this kind are recent and ongoing. By no means all the factors affecting our usage in conversation are known. But it is such work that illustrates the empirical contribution of linguistics to language study.

The *theoretical* contribution of linguistics, referred to above, now needs further discussion, in that unless we can grasp in broad outline a picture of the way in which language is structured, it will be very difficult to find our way about the subject. We need a model of the main branches of the discipline of linguistics as a preliminary to any more detailed study. Figure 1 therefore shows one possible model of language structure, which attempts to interrelate the main branches of the discipline.

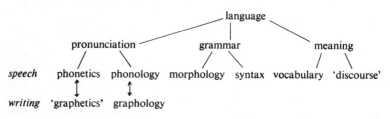

Figure 1   Levels of language

There are of course many possible models of the structure of language, and each has its controversial points; but all accounts agree that certain components are essential, and the figure illustrates what these are. For speech, which is the primary medium of normal human language, three main components, or *levels* of structure are recognized: pronunciation, grammar and meaning. (This is by no means a novel analysis, of course: distinctions of this kind were made by traditional grammarians too.) 'Pronunciation' is, however, too broad a notion to be left as it is. There are two aspects to its study. Firstly, we may study the properties of human soundmaking as such—the way in which we

---

[5] For a fuller discussion of these features, see Crystal and Davy, *Advanced conversational English*, chapter 3.

form, transmit and hear sounds. This is the subject of *phonetics*. Apart from certain medical conditions (e.g. cleft palate), all human beings are born with the same vocal apparatus, and in principle can make the same range of sounds. Because of its general applicability, therefore— providing a means of analysing and transcribing the speech of the speakers of any language—the subject is sometimes called 'general phonetics'. It has to be clearly distinguished from the second term under the heading of pronunciation, 'Phonology'. Phonology is primarily the study of the sound system of a particular language, such as English or French. Out of the great range of sounds it is possible for each of us to produce, we in fact only use a small set of sounds in our own language—some 40-odd distinctive sound-units, or phonemes, in the case of English, for instance. Whereas phonetics studies pronunciation in general, therefore, phonology studies the pronunciation system of a particular language, aiming ultimately at establishing linguistic principles which will explain the differences and similarities between all such systems.[6]

A similar distinction might be made for the written medium, represented further down the diagram. Here we are all familiar with the idea of a language's spelling and punctuation system. The study of such things, and the analysis of the principles underlying writing systems in general, is equivalent to investigating the phonology of speech, and is sometimes called 'graphology' accordingly. Each language has its own graphological system. One might also recognize a subject analogous to phonetics (say, 'graphetics') which studied the properties of human mark-making: the range of marks it is possible to make on a range of surfaces using a range of implements, and the way in which these marks are visually perceived. This is hardly a well-defined subject as yet, hence my inverted commas, but it is beginning to be studied: typographers look at some aspects of the problem, as do educational psychologists. From the linguistic point of view, it should be possible to establish a basic alphabet of shapes that could be said to underlie the various alphabets of the world—just as there is a basic international phonetic alphabet of sounds. But this is a field still in its infancy.

On the right of the diagram we see the study of meaning, or 'semantics'. In a full account, this branch would need many subdivisions, but I will mention only two. The first is the study of the meaning of words, under the heading of 'vocabulary', or 'lexis'. This is the familiar aspect of the study of meaning, as it provides the content of dictionaries. But of course there is far more to meaning than the study of individual words. We may talk about the distribution of meaning in a sentence, a paragraph (topic sentences, for instance), in a chapter, and so on. Such broader aspects of meaning have been little studied in a scientific way,

[6] See further J. D. O'Connor, *Phonetics* (Penguin 1973).

but they need a place in our model of language. I refer to them using the label 'discourse'—but as this term is not as universally accepted as the others in my diagram, I have left inverted commas around it.[7]

Sounds on the left; meanings on the right. 'Grammar', in the centre of the model, is appropriately placed, for it has traditionally been viewed as the central, organizing principle of language—the way in which sounds and meanings are related. It is often referred to simply as 'structure'. There are naturally many conceptions as to how the grammatical basis of a language is best studied; and comparing the various schools of thought (transformational grammar, systemic grammar, and so on) forms much of the content of introductory linguistics courses. But one particularly well-established distinction is that between 'morphology' and 'syntax', and that is presented in the model. Morphology is the study of the structure of words: how they are built up, using roots, prefixes, suffixes, and so on—*nation, national, nationalize* etc., or *walk, walks, walking, walked*. Syntax is the study of the way words work in sequences to form larger linguistic units: phrases, clauses, sentences and beyond. For most linguists, syntax is, in effect, the study of sentence structure; but the syntactic structure of discourse is, as we have already seen, also an important topic.[8]

All schools of thought in linguistics recognize the usefulness of the concepts of pronunciation, grammar and meaning, and the main-subdivisions these contain, though they approach their study in different ways. Some insist on the study of meaning before all else, for example; others on the study of grammar first. But the existence of such differences should not blind us to the considerable overlap between them. However, before we can claim that our model is in any sense a complete account of the main branches of language, useful as a perspective for applied language work, we have to insert three further dimensions. These are to take account of the fact of language variation. Any instance of language has a structure represented by the model in figure 1; but over and above this, we have to recognize the existence of different kinds of language being used in different kinds of situation. Basically, there are three types of variation, due to historical, social and psychological factors. These are represented in figure 2. 'Historical linguistics' describes and explains the facts of language change through time, and this provides our model with an extra dimension. But at any point in time, language varies from one social situation to another: there are regional dialects of English, social dialects, and many other styles, as has already been mentioned. 'Sociolinguistics' is the study of the way language varies in relation to social situations, and is becoming an increasingly important part of the subject as a whole. It too requires

[7] See further F. R. Palmer, *Semantics* (Cambridge University Press 1975).
[8] See further F. R. Palmer, *Grammar* (Penguin 1971).

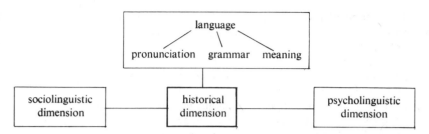

Figure 2   Main dimensions of language variation

a separate dimension. And lastly, 'psycholinguistics' is the study of language variation in relation to thinking and to other psychological processes within the individual—in particular, to the way in which language development and use is influenced by—or influences—such factors as memory, attention and perception.[9]

At this point any initial perspective has to stop. From now on, we would be involved in a more detailed study of the aims of the various branches outlined, and we would have to investigate further different theoretical conceptions, techniques, terminology and so on. This can be done by means of the further reading given below (p. 32). But it should be clear from what has been said so far that in providing a precise and coherent way of identifying and discussing the complex facts of language structure and use, the potential applicability of the subject is very great. What must be remembered in particular is the distinction between (a) the need to get a sense of the subject of language as a whole, and (b) the mastery of a particular model of analysis to aid in a specific analytical or experimental task. Everything in the present chapter might be summarized as an attempt to illustrate a linguistic 'state of mind', a way of looking at language that can provide fresh or revealing facts or explanations about the structure and use of language. If the examples have been interesting, then this in itself might be justification for further study of the subject. What would then be involved would be a more detailed examination of some of the main theoretical principles that underlie any scientific study of language, such as the distinction between historical and non-historical (diachronic v. synchronic) modes of language study, the distinction between language form and language content, and the importance of language variety.

[9] Introductions to the more detailed study of these dimensions are P. Trudgill, *Sociolinguistics: an introduction* (Penguin 1974); G. Turner, *Stylistics* (Penguin 1973); D. I. Slobin, *Psycholinguistics* (Glenview, Illinois, Scott Foresman 1971); W. P. Lehmann, *Historical linguistics: an introduction* (New York, Holt, Rinehart and Winston 1962). Specifically on English, see R. Quirk, *The use of English* (2nd edition, Longman 1968); B. Foster, *The changing English language* (Penguin 1970).

In the light of these principles, old problems turn up in a new light, and a certain amount of rethinking about traditional ideas becomes necessary.

Such rethinking can proceed along two lines, a general and a particular. The general viewpoint tends to give rise to fierce debate, and I shall postpone discussion of it until chapter 3: this is the need to develop greater *tolerance* of language varieties and uses—of other people's accent and dialect, in particular. Can this be done without sacrificing the notion of the 'standard' language, without losing a sense of 'correctness' in language use, and all that many would hold dear? The criticisms that linguists have made of purism, cited above, have sometimes led people to accuse linguistics of throwing all standards to the winds—of wanting to say that 'anything goes', that it does not matter how we speak or write, as long as we are intelligible, expressing our ideas, and so on. This is simply not so. The point is taken up on p. 70.

The 'particular' viewpoint can be illustrated here, however, because it shows the kind of detailed thinking that needs to take place in adopting a linguistic way of looking at language. We may take any of the traditional grammatical categories, such as 'number', 'person', 'tense' or 'case' to demonstrate this. Traditionally, it was assumed that there existed a neat one-to-one relationship between the formal category and its meaning, viz. singular = 'one', plural = 'more than one'; 1st person = 'me' or 'us', 2nd person = 'you', 3rd person = 'the other person(s)'; tense = time; genitive case = possession. One of the things that linguistics has tried to do is show how such neat equations do not work. In the person system, for example, we can show this complexity very readily. Taking just one form (the so-called 'first person') we find that the *we* form *may* refer to the 1st person (as in 'We are going', where it refers to the speaker along with someone else), but it may also be used to refer to the 2nd person (as when a nurse addresses a patient with a 'how are we today?' where the *we* is equivalent to 'you'), or to the 3rd person (as when one secretary asks another 'how are we today', gesturing at their boss who has just gone into his office).

Another example of unexpected complexity is the tense system. There are many problems in the view that tense expresses time, and that time relationships are expressed by tense forms only. Visualizing time as a line,

past time	now	future time

it might seem plausible to see the tenses fitting in neatly, as follows:

PAST	PRESENT	FUTURE
(*I walked/was walking*)	(*I walk/am walking*)	(*I will walk/be walking*)
past time	now	future time

But there are many examples of usage where this parallelism does not work. For instance, the present tense form *may* refer to present time, as in *I'm leaving*. But it may also help to refer to future time, when used with a future adverbial, as in *I'm going to town tomorrow*; or to past time, when used with a past narrative marker, e.g. *Three weeks ago, I'm walking down this road . . .*; or to habitual action, when used with an adverbial of frequency (*I go to town three times a week*); or to very recent time (as in news headlines, e.g. *Sir X dies*); or to no time at all (the so-called 'timeless' present, as in *Oil floats on water*). Similar examples would arise if we were to consider the other tense forms.

It should be noticed how an examination of just one small area of grammar involves the use of a number of technical terms (even though the meanings of these terms are fairly obvious). It is evident that the need to talk at this level of detail is not far away, as soon as we approach any area of grammar. It is easy to make general, impressionistic remarks about children's usage, for example—about the 'complexity' of their sentences, or about their use of tenses or adjectives or prepositions. But such general remarks need to be carefully watched (as in the example of proper and common nouns, p. 18). And indeed, most of the 'obvious' features of language emerge as hiding considerable complexity, when they are subjected to analysis. Two further examples will illustrate this: the blind use of the idea of 'parts of speech', and an uncritical acceptance of measures of 'length'. The notion of 'parts of speech', for instance, seems easy enough to apply, as long as we are dealing with nouns, verbs, and other central classes. It is less easy to use when classifying such words as *yes, please, sorry, not*, and cases where words have several different uses. And we must remember that definitions of even the central classes can vary greatly from book to book. The notion of 'sentence length' provides another example of hidden complexity. This is a concept commonly used as a means of plotting language development—sentences get longer as children grow older. But how exactly is length to be measured—in syllables, words, phrases . . .? If words, then would we count *it's* as one word or two? Would idioms (such as *it's raining cats and dogs*) be counted as having the same number of 'units' as literal sentences (such as *he's keeping cats and dogs*)? And what would we say about two sentences that were equal in length but which differed markedly in complexity (e.g. *The man and the dog and the cat were tired* and *The dog belonging to the man was in the kitchen*)? Such questions immediately arise as soon as we try to work with a simple measure of length.

Last of all—that is, after we have been motivated to accept the *general* aims and tenets of linguistic inquiry—there is the need to find and use a specific *model* of linguistic description, in order to interrelate our various observations about language structure and use. Whatever our aims (whether assessment, screening, remediation, development . . .)

the need for a standard descriptive measure is paramount. There is no point in describing child A in terms of one linguistic framework, child B in terms of another, and then hoping to compare the two. (This is similar to—but infinitely more complex than—comparing two objects using two systems of measurement: if one is 16 centimetres and the other 11 inches, which is the longer?) This point is taken up in chapter 3. Likewise, an inventory, or list of 'noticeable' or 'interesting' features in someone's use of language is not an adequate account of it, and may mislead. The dangers of 'selective commentary' are threefold. (a) We tend to notice only what we have been trained to look for, e.g. pronouns, adjectives, tense forms; (b) some of the most important features of language may be omitted because they are not readily noticeable, e.g. variations in word order, elliptical patterns; and (c) an inventory provides no explanation, or sense of underlying pattern—for example, to make a list of features, in which item 13 was the definite article, and item 73 the indefinite article, would obviously be of little value. At some point in any grammar of English, these two items would have to be brought together, because the meaning of the one helps to establish the meaning of the other. And so it is for most areas of grammar. Grammar is not a random collection of features, nor is it learned in this way (see chapter 2), and the same applies to other levels of language also. It is the task of the linguist to define all the variables that make up the language *system*, and say how they relate to each other. Naturally, with such a complex system as language, there is no obvious 'best' way of doing this, and this is why there are so many competing linguistic theories. Each tries to present an explanation of language which models the way in which the system 'works'. Thus one encounters the 'generative' schools of thought associated with Chomsky, those associated with M. A. K. Halliday (first 'scale-and-category' grammar, later 'systemic' grammar), and so on. At some stage the student of language has to come to grips with one of them, and learn to use it confidently, in order to provide himself with a framework in principle consistent and comprehensive for carrying out his language tasks. This is no place to argue the merits and demerits of the different positions: each model has its strengths and insights, each its weaknesses and obscurities. But there is no avoiding this final jump. Without a fund of formal knowledge to back up our general knowledge of linguistic aims and theory, there can be no bridge between beliefs and practice. If the reader has accepted the argument so far, then he will not find it difficult to get detailed information about the kinds of bridge that are available.[10] In chapter 3 I look at what happens if this bridge is not built.

[10] See further D. Bolinger, *Aspects of language* (2nd edition, New York, Harcourt, Brace and World 1975), J. Lyons, *Chomsky* (London, Fontana 1970), J. Lyons (ed.), *New horizons in linguistics* (Penguin 1970).

Chapter 2 Language acquisition

So far, I have been arguing for a realistic awareness of the nature of the adult language and a principled approach to the analysis of it. The importance of conversational data, in particular, emerged. Only with this as a perspective—the normal conversational interaction of the home background, and the possibility of a systematic and comprehensive analysis of it—can we hope to evaluate a child upon his arrival in school (see further chapter 3). But now we must move on to a consideration of normal child language development, the second stage in the general argument outlined in the Introduction. This is necessary because it is an essential preliminary to any arguments involving the teaching of reading, the practice of therapy, or programmes of special education. What, then, is known of the acquisition of language in children?

The contemporary study of the acquisition of language by children has arisen out of the overlapping interests of psychologist and linguist. The role of language in relation to child development and cognition has always been recognized as one of psychology's prime concerns. What has now been found is that the assumptions, techniques and findings of modern linguistics can contribute greatly towards defining and solving the problems encountered in this area, and presenting a more systematic and coherent view of the whole. It is this blend of linguistic and psychological insight that identifies current work in language acquisition.

The contribution of linguistics has been recent but decisive. The first detailed projects were produced in the early 1960s, by Roger Brown and others, but they were followed by a veritable flood of publications, some of which are give below.[1] Throughout this work we can see linguistics making a contribution in the same three areas as those discussed in chapter 1: the theoretical, the methodological and the empirical. Each of these emphases will be illustrated in the present

---

[1] An account of this work is well reflected in R. Brown, *A first language* (Cambridge, Massachusetts, Harvard University Press 1973). Reviews of the literature are included in such introductions as P. Menyuk, *The acquisition and development of language* (Englewood Cliffs, New Jersey, Prentice-Hall 1971), and P. Dale, *Language development: structure and function* (Holt, Rinehart and Winston 1972). Current trends are reflected in the *Journal of Child Language* (Cambridge University Press).

chapter, but as it is the recent theoretical discussion which has the broadest implications, I shall begin with this.

By the theoretical contribution of linguistics in this area, I am referring to the discussion which has gone on about the structure and function of language that has enabled us to see the kind of principles which could explain the facts of language development. Why do children acquire language in the way they do, at the speed they do? Are there common patterns of development in all children? The classical explanation of language learning was that it was essentially a process of imitation and reinforcement. The child learned to speak by copying the noise-patterns heard around him, and through stimulus and response, trial and error, reinforcement and reward, he would refine his own production until it matched the language of his adult models. Chomsky and others, working within the framework of generative grammar, were the first to discuss at length various fallacies in this *behaviourist* account of the language-acquisition process.[2] Two arguments are particularly crucial. On the one hand, if imitation were the governing principle, then we would expect children to produce rather different patterns in their language than in fact they do. On the other hand, we would expect them *not* to produce some of the patterns that in fact they come out with. Let us take these two points separately: first, the argument that children do not produce what we would expect from an imitation hypothesis.

This is clear from the end of the first year, when, if imitation were all that were involved, we would expect children to produce far more in the way of adult baby-talk than they do. The 'Isn't he a lovely little baba den' kind of language is a dominant feature of the child's environment over the first twelve months, and it is marked by distinctive intonational and tone-of-voice patterns. We would expect these to be picked up and used by the child, but the characteristic intonation patterns of the one-year-old do not display such distinctive patterns. Imitation obviously plays an important role in the development of pronunciation (see p. 41), but it is not the whole story. Another example comes from later development, around age three-and-a-half. If imitation is the norm, then we would expect a child who has made a mistake in grammar, and who is being corrected by his mother, to pick up and use the correction fairly quickly. But he does not do so. One dialogue, taken from a report by David McNeill, illustrates this.[3] Here, the child was apparently unable to use a pattern, even though presented with the correct adult model (for that dialect) several times. The child began

[2] See, for example, Chomsky's review of B. F. Skinner, in *Language* 35 (1959), 26–58.
[3] In 'Developmental psycholinguistics', in F. Smith and G. A. Miller (eds.), *The genesis of language* (Cambridge, Massachusetts, Massachusetts Institute of Technology Press 1966), 69.

by saying 'Nobody don't like me.' The mother corrected, with 'No, say nobody like*s* me.' The child ignored, saying 'Nobody don't like me.' This dialogue was repeated eight times, presumably to a point of exasperation, and concluded with the impatient outburst, 'Oh! Nobody don't likes me.' One conclusion to be drawn from this is that the child was not at this point in its development ready to use the negative pattern expected in this dialect of English. It suggests, in other words, that language acquisition is more a matter of maturation of the child's own internal grammar than one of imitation. (I recall Harold Rosen in a lecture once making various caustic comments about the mother in this example also, in relation to the *ego* image being reinforced in the child. Nobody seems to be disagreeing that nobody likes him!)

The second argument referred to above was that if imitation were a sufficient explanation, we would not be able to explain some of the things that children actually do in their utterances. The best example of this is the process often labelled 'analogy'. The child who says 'I goed' instead of 'I went', or 'mouses' instead of 'mice' has not obtained these patterns from any adult model. What he has done is produce new forms by extending his understanding of the regular patterns of the language. All children seem to assume that language is regular, to begin with: they then have to learn, slowly and painfully, that it is not. In this case, the child knows that one says 'boy' and 'boys', 'bus' and 'buses', and so on: he therefore assumes that one also says 'mouse' and 'mouses'. Far from this being an error, to be criticized, the production of such forms is one of the most important stages in normal language development: it shows that the child is adopting an intelligent, deductive, creative role towards his language. And it suggests, along with the other evidence, that an explanation for the facts of language development must lie elsewhere than under the heading of imitation.

What alternative is there, then? The alternative proposed by Chomsky and others is that the child is born with an innate capacity for language development; that the human being is in some way pre-structured towards the development of language, so that when the child is exposed to language, certain language-structuring principles automatically commence to operate. The model that is used to indicate what is going on is that of the 'Language Acquisition Device' (LAD). This device is essentially a hypothesis about those features of the structure of language which are progressively used as the child matures—structural information, perhaps, such as that people speak in sentences, or that sentences have two basic parts, subject and predicate (or actor and action). In outline, its operation can be seen in figure 3. The speech patterns in the child's environment constitute the primary linguistic data used as input to the child. The LAD then suggests how the child operates on this input, deriving from it hypotheses about the grammar of the language—what the sentences are, where the actor of a sentence is,

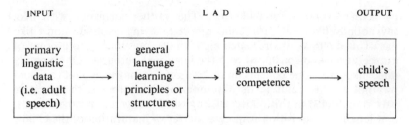

Figure 3   Generative model of language acquisition

and so on. In one language, say English, this 'scanning' would result in a conclusion that subjects go *before* the verbs; in some other language, say Welsh, the same scanning would produce the reverse conclusion, that subjects go after verbs. In some such way as this, the child accumulates specific information about the grammatical structure of his own language using these general, or universal principles. The acquisition of this grammatical competence would of course emerge in his production of sentences that correspond to adult speech (though only after a process of trial and error, showing that he is constantly revising his hypotheses about what the language is like). In other words, his output ends up identical with the input.

Only by postulating such a device, it is argued, can we explain the facts that an imitation theory cannot explain, and many other facts besides. Facts such as the remarkable rapidity with which children learn the basic structures of their language: by three-and-a-half, after all, most of the sentence patterns of the language have been acquired (see p. 47). Or facts such as the broadly similar order of acquisition of various structures observed among different children (see p. 50). If there is a common order of acquisition for structures, then this could be taken as evidence in support of an internal process of language maturation. But of course there is a long way to go before such ideas as the Language Acquisition Device become convincing. The precise nature of any innate principle needs to be much more precisely defined, and it is difficult to see how this might be done in a scientifically testable way, in the present state of knowledge. Or again, if there are innate principles, then these must apply to all speakers of all languages: it would therefore follow that the languages of the world will all be acquired along broadly similar lines. There is some evidence for this,[4] but so few languages have yet been studied in detail that conclusions must remain extremely tentative at present. In other words, while the

---

[4] See, for example, the general discussion of universals in D. I. Slobin, 'Cognitive prerequisites for the development of grammar', in C. A. Ferguson and D. I. Slobin (eds.), *Studies of child language development* (Holt, Rinehart and Winston 1973), 175–208.

theoretical issues posed by the facts of language acquisition have been defined more clearly by the psycholinguistic debate, few generally agreed answers have been arrived at. Both maturation and imitation are factors affecting the acquisition of language, it is clear, but the precise interrelationship between the two is quite uncertain. What is needed, evidently, is large-scale empirical and methodological research into a wide range of children across a wide range of languages.

There are in any case many other theories which have been proposed in order to explain the observed regularities in the order of acquisition of linguistic features. Perhaps the most influential at present is the view derived from the Genevan psychologist, Jean Piaget, who argues that language must be viewed within the context of the child's cognitive development as a whole. Linguistic structures will emerge only if the intellectual and other psychological preconditions are right. For example, if the child is to acquire the comparative structure (e.g. *This box has more apples in it than that box*), he must be able to handle the conceptual tasks involved, such as quantification and comparison. Piaget proposes several very broad stages of cognitive development. So far however, there have been few experimental studies of the way in which linguistic features can be shown to relate to these stages, and as yet the detailed relevance of Piaget's principles remains uncertain. It would in fact be premature to commit ourselves to *any* one general theory of language acquisition. It is even premature to assume that a single explanation may run the whole way through the acquisition process. It is perfectly conceivable to think of language acquisition as a blend of *different* learning principles and strategies that operate at different stages of development. Imitation, for example, may be relatively unimportant at one stage, but crucial at another; it may be difficult to use in explaining the acquisition of grammatical structure, but it may be easier to use in explaining the acquisition of vocabulary; and so on.[5] With so few children from so few languages having been studied, it is too soon to be able to resolve such issues.

The point was made above that there are certain broad similarities in the manner in which language is acquired. Until more languages are studied, it is impossible to say how many such 'universals' there might be, but enough information has been collected for English to make certain generalizations possible—at least about the acquisition of phonology and grammar (the development of semantic and socio-linguistic abilities is still largely unclear, though this is where the bulk of contemporary research is located). There is considerable evidence to support the view that the sounds and structures of English develop on similar lines for all children, in the sense that the *order* in which

---

[5] This topic is reviewed in R. Clark, 'What's the use of imitation?' *Journal of Child Language* 4 (forthcoming).

they are mastered is common to all. In pronunciation, for example, certain categories of sound will be discriminated and will be produced before others: it would be improbable to find a child for whom consonants such as /s/ or /z/ were being systematically produced before consonants such as /m/ or /d/, for instance. Likewise in grammar, all children begin with simple one-word utterances (e.g. *dada!*) and proceed in stages to more complex sentence types (see below). But before giving details, it is important to stress that postulating a common order does not imply an identical *rate* of development. On the contrary, it is a commonplace that there may be very great differences in the speed at which a given linguistic feature is acquired, within the spectrum of 'normal' children. All kinds of factors are involved, affecting the quantity as well as the quality of a child's comprehension or production (e.g. socioeconomic background, sex, intelligence, opportunity, motivation), though few have been systematically studied (the evidence is however fairly behind the view that girls, on the whole, learn linguistic features in advance of boys). This variability does not disallow talking of stages of chronological development, as long as the potential extent of the variation in rate is taken into account. Whenever an age is given below, therefore, I assume that within the range of 'normal' development a variation of anything up to $\pm$ 6 months is quite to be expected.

Phonology
Several studies have been made of the order of events in the acquisition of phonology, though no completely satisfactory explanation of these observed sequences has yet been agreed. But in general outline, it is evident that a number of stages are involved.

(*1*)   Between birth and around 6 months, children use a series of nonlinguistic, biologically-conditioned vocalizations, ranging from early cries of hunger, pain, pleasure etc., through the 'cooing' of around 3 months, to the more well-defined sounds of babbling, from around 6 months. The important point to note here is that this is not a linguistic stage, as far as the production of the sounds is concerned. A comparison of babies from different language backgrounds would show no influence of the mother-tongue. (And it has often been noted that deaf babies also produce vocalizations that are very similar to those of hearing children, at this stage.)

(*2*)   Between 6 and 9 months, the vocalization begins to take on some of the characteristics of a specific language, as features of pitch (intonation), rhythm and tone of voice come to be used. Such language-specific features may have been understood and responded to much earlier, of course (as early as 2–3 months, according to some studies), but production of these features is not apparent in any systematic way until the second half of the first year.[6] The intonation will then have both an emotional role, expressing the child's attitudes, as well as an important grammatical role—it provides a means of organizing the vocalizations into units within which sentence patterns will ultimately emerge. Parental reactions such as 'He always says that when he sees his teddy', or 'He's trying to tell us something' indicate the way in which we gradually become aware of an organization being imposed on babbling. By 12 months, most children have developed this ability to great lengths, being able to carry on primitive conversations with their parents, in which their entire utterance is unintelligible except for the earnestness of the intonation. Such 'scribble-talk', or 'jargon' (as it is referred to within speech therapy) may have little within it capable of being identified with the words, consonants or vowels of English; it is however clearly English in its prosody. And it is, accordingly, during this stage that it is possible to begin telling children of different language backgrounds apart, on the basis of their utterance (and also possible to detect the onset of the 'deaf voice' of the child with a profound hearing loss, as it is at this point that his disability will affect the phonetic characteristics of his output).

(*3*)   From 9 months, it becomes increasingly possible to identify segments of vocalization that seem to correspond to words. The way in which a child progresses from babbling to meaningful speech is not totally understood: some stop babbling before they begin to talk; others continue to babble long after; others develop 'transitional' stages, or mix babbling and wordlike units in certain ways.[7] By around 12 months, most children have come to produce at least one unit with a stable pronunciation and a regular interpretation—the so-called 'first word'. About this notion, however, a number of points need to be made. Firstly, it is misleading to think of this first word as the place where language development starts, i.e. around 12 months. Rather, a great deal of language production has been taking place already, especially in the learning of the prosodic framework within which the word will be uttered. Also, from the point of view of comprehension, the child must be said to have been acquiring his language for several months previously. The emphasis on 'first words' is a little misplaced, too, because so much depends for their identification on the abilities of the parents. The early pronunciation attempts at words like *dada* or *there* may be quite unlike the 'correct' pronunciations. Some parents seem

[6] See D. Crystal, 'Non-segmental phonology in language acquisition', in *The English tone of voice*, 96–104.
[7] See further N. S. Rees, 'The role of babbling in the child's acquisition of language', *British Journal of Disorders of Communication* 7 (1972), 17–23; J. Dore, M. B. Franklin, R. T. Miller and A. Ramer, 'Transitional phenomena in early language acquisition', *Journal of Child Language* 3 (1976), 13–28.

very good at detecting and interpreting such 'proto-words'; others seem very poor. The shout of recognition that goes with the first word, in short, tells us more about the abilities of the parents than about those of the child!

Secondly, the 'first word' is hardly a word at all, if by that we mean the adult conception of a word, as given, say, in a dictionary. The child's units of meaning often correspond to stretches of speech that to the adult would be more than one word, e.g. *allgone, gimme*, and *restego* (one child's attempt at the jumping game 'ready-steady-go' played with his father, which he subsequently used as a verb—'you stego with me now'). Nor is the meaning necessarily anything like the adult's meaning. On the contrary, the meaning of the child's early words is usually much more diffuse—'over-extended' in meaning, as the acquisition literature puts it. *Dada* is not easily definable as 'my male parent', for example. The child may be seen using it and pointing at his daddy, but invariably the word is used in other contexts also, e.g. referring to the milkman, or pointing to the sweet tin. On the basis of such usage, it is clear that the word is being used in a very broad sense, expressing more a sense of 'want' or 'pleasant experience' than that of 'father'.[8] Another example was the word *door*, said while pointing at the door. We might be forgiven for thinking that the child meant 'door', but the trouble was that when the door was open this child would not accept the label *door* used with reference to it. *Door* was also used pointing at a drawer, and then to a pocket into which a handkerchief had just been placed. It became apparent that the meaning of door was 'shut away'—only shut, closed or hidden things were 'doors'. In other words, this 'noun' had been given a sense that was almost that of a verb—referring more to an action than an object.

Thirdly, a 'word' at this stage, seen as a recognizable lexical item, is also made to function in a variety of sentence-like ways. In the case of one child, the word *dada* (this time, in the sense of 'father') was observed to be used in several distinct ways: with a definite, falling intonation, often accompanied by a pointing gesture, to mean something like 'there's daddy'; *dadá*, said with a rising intonation, to express a querulous or puzzled attitude; and *dadà*, with a heavily stressed level or falling second syllable, often accompanied by arms outstretched, to mean 'I want daddy'. It is tempting to conclude that here the intonation and gesture add up to the use of statements, questions and commands; but while there is a certain semantic resemblance, it would be misleading to say that the child has learned the grammar of English in these respects. Terms like 'statement' and 'question' are properly used only when the syntax develops sufficiently to enable us to see the difference

[8] See R. Jakobson, 'Why "mama" and "papa"?' in *Selected writings* (The Hague, Mouton 1962), 538–45.

in word-endings or word-order. Intonation and gesture, at this stage, are extremely ambiguous and indeterminate features of expression: a rising tone does *not* always mean 'question'; it may also mean 'irritated statement' or 'grim command', or a host of other attitudes. To conclude, then, that when a child says *dada*, he is 'really' saying 'Is that dada?', only omitting the first two words, is to attribute more linguistic knowledge to the child than he probably possesses. All we can say with confidence is that *dada* is being used as a one-element sentence (for which the term *holophrase* has sometimes been used). In other words, the 'first words' are really 'first sentences', though they lack the specific structure and function that we come to associate with the syntactically developed sentences of later life (discussed further below).

(*4*)   Once a systematic use of words is established, it is possible to talk about the learning of the units of the pronunciation system of the language (the *phonemes*). During the babbling period, several sounds will have been used, but as already pointed out these are sounds used in a nonlinguistic way; their function is not to show differences between meanings (as with *pin, pen, bin, big, beg* etc.), and they are therefore not part of the sound system of English. Once the child begins to learn the use of sound contrastively for semantic purposes (towards the end of the first year), then he begins to build up his sound system from scratch, and whatever sounds he may previously have used in his bab-bling (or, sometimes, will *still be* using in his babble) are strictly irrelevant to understanding how he does this. To miss this distinction, between the sounds (phonetics) of babbling and the sound-contrasts (phonology) of speech, can lead to serious confusion. Some children, for example, babble a wide range of sounds including some that seem like *s, l,* and *r.* Later, when their babbling dies away, and they begin to build up their phonological system, the contrast in 'fluency' may be remarkable. To parents, it may sound as if their child has stopped talking. 'He had all kinds of consonants and vowels a few weeks ago, but now he has none—only *dada*' is the kind of comment heard. The fallacy is in thinking of babbling as if it were language, as having con-sonants, vowels, and so on. It does not. The child is certainly practising the making of sounds, but he is not consciously organizing them in a meaningful way. When faced with the problem of communicating meaningfully, he then has to learn how to use sounds systematically. His babbling period, it is thought, provides an important practice stage in this process, but it must not be taken for the real thing, speech.

The learning of the sound system of a language, then, begins at around 9 months, with the child beginning to discriminate and produce the vowel and consonant phonemes of the language, in the many contexts in which they occur. It is a long process, that is not completed until around 7 years of age. It is also a complicated process, that is not fully understood, though several stages of development are apparent, and some of the processes which govern development are known. In addition, we may state with confidence that certain things do *not* happen. For example, it is not possible to generalize about the order in which children pick up the actual *sounds* of the language: no two children that have been studied have been identical in every respect. Some start with a *p* sound (along with a vowel), some with *m*, some with *d*, and so on. On the other hand, it does seem possible to suggest certain general tendencies, based on the *type* of sound that is produced, and taking into account the fact that some sounds are more audible than others (e.g. [a] over [i], vowels over consonants), some are more difficult to produce than others (e.g. consonant clusters over consonants; [r] or [z] over [t] or [f]), some are more frequently used than others (e.g. [t], [s]), and so on. For example, it has been suggested that children tend to use front consonants (like *p, b, m,*) before back (like *k, g*); plosives (like *p, b*) before fricatives (like *f, v, s, z*); and oral sounds (like *d, g*) before their nasal equivalents (like *n, ng*). Syllables will begin by being Consonant + Vowel in structure (so-called 'open' syllables); clusters of consonants will tend to appear at the ends of words (as in *cats, jump*) before the beginnings (as in *stick, train*); and so on. A diagram which orders the appearance of consonant phonemes in English with respect to chronological age is as follows:

By 2	p b m n w
2½	t d k g ŋ (as in si*ng*) h
3	f s l y (as in *y*ou)
4	ʃ (as in *sh*ip) v z r tʃ (as in *ch*ew) dʒ (as in *j*uice)
5	θ (as in *th*ink) ð (as in *th*is)
6	ʒ (as in mea*s*ure)

Figure 4   Average age estimates for the acquisition of English consonants.[9]

Any such diagram, it is clear, omits a great deal, and is misleading in its simplicity. Figure 4 says nothing about where in a word the phonemes are used. or how accurately they are pronounced; it says nothing about which phonemes children have difficulty discriminating; nor about the nature of any general processes which may govern the way in which these sounds are strung together into sequences (e.g. the 'reduplicative' pattern of early syllable sequences, such as *baba, dada, tete*); nor about the types of simplification of complex sounds which

[9] This diagram is a synthesis of several accounts. See E. K. Sander, 'When are speech sounds learned?' *Journal of Speech and Hearing Disorders* 37 (1961), 55–63; D. Olmsted, Out of the mouth of babes (Mouton 1971); and the reports in D. Ingram, *Phonological disability in children* (Edward Arnold 1976), chapter 2.

these phonemes may represent (e.g. *slide* becoming *'lide*, *train* becoming *tain*, *this* becoming *dis*). In particular, the diagram says nothing about how long it takes to 'acquire' a sound. It may in fact take a very long time between the stage when a child first tries out a new sound in a word to the stage where (a) he consistently uses that sound every time he uses that word, and (b) he uses that sound in all the words where an adult would use it. A 5-year-old who has no trouble with *b* in words like *bin* and *rob* (where the contrasts with such words as *pin* and *rock* is straightforward) may none the less replace *b* by another sound in contexts where the contrast is not needed, e.g. 'disturv' for *disturb*. And this leads to a further general point, namely, that just because a child uses a sound apparently correctly does not mean that he is able to distinguish that sound from all the others in the language. It has in fact been shown that some consonant contrasts (the difference between the front fricatives *f* and *th*, for example) cause difficulty until 7 years or beyond—that is, words distinguished only by these may be confused.[10]

(5)   Most of the phonological system has been acquired by the time the child is 5, therefore, but certain features take longer. The discrimination of front fricatives is one example of a problem that most primary school children have, regardless of the accent they happen to have. Another problem is in the production of the more complex consonant clusters in the language, e.g. *strength*, *twelfths*, where substitutions and omissions are typical until quite late on. Many of the more subtle uses of intonation are also not acquired until late—as late as 10 years, in some instances. For example, there is the use of intonation to express contrastive emphasis in certain kinds of structure, e.g. *John gave a book to Jim and he gave one to Mary* (where John gave the book to Mary), compared with *John gave a book to Jim and HE gave one to Mary* (where Jim gave the book to Mary). This contrast would still cause most 8–9 year-olds trouble. A recent experiment[11] showed how it was not until around 10 years that the intonations of reinforcements, diminution and equivalence were fully appreciated. The context chosen for study was that of football results being read aloud. The contrasts are usually clear, typified by:

Everton ⌃1, Lïverpool   (a draw)

Everton ⌃1, Lïverpool   (an away win)

Everton ⌃1, Lïverpool   (a home win)

[10] See Ingram, *op. cit.*, chapter 2, and M. L. Edwards, 'Perception and production in child phonology: the testing of four hypotheses', *Journal of Child Language* 1 (1974), 205–19.

[11] A. Cruttenden, 'An experiment involving comprehension of intonation in children from 7 to 10', *Journal of Child Language* 1 (1974), 221–31.

It is possible to predict the second result on the basis of the 'expectant' intonation of the first three words (e.g. the high falling–rising tone implying something 'extra', the 'sad' diminishing tone implying something 'less'). The interesting point is that (even football-crazy) 7-year-olds are unable to predict results in this way; whereas by 10 years, this was being done fairly routinely.

Grammar

In much the same way, it is possible to hypothesize several stages through which children seem to pass in acquiring the grammar of their language. Once again, the qualifications made above about chronological variation and the reading in of meaning apply. The latter point is particularly important in relation to grammar. It is very tempting to take a child's primitive sentences and assume that he really knows the adult version, but is limited in his ability to speak it. For instance, a child who says *Man walking shops* might be interpreted as 'saying' 'The man is walking to the shops.' It may be clear from the context that this is what he intended (though it often is not—the same context might equally well have inspired 'The man is walking near the shops', and many other interpretations); but even so, it would still be fallacious to say that the child has 'left out' some of the words in such sentences. If the child never uses words like *the*, *is* or *to*, then how could we possibly tell that they were there—only 'beneath the surface', as it were? It is no answer to say, 'Because he understands them in the adults' speech', as there is no clear way of demonstrating this either. No experiment has yet been devised which can take a 2-year-old and present him with contrasts between *to the shops* and *near the shops*—or *any* such contrasts —so that he will show he can tell the difference in meaning. The problems are largely practical ones, of controlling the child, and presenting the experimental tasks in a comprehensible way; but they are enormous. Until such time, then, as it is possible to prove that comprehension of the 'omitted' features of grammar exists in the child's mind, there is no justification for attributing any grammatical abilities to the child other than those for which there is clear formal evidence in his actual usage, such as a contrast between two word-orders correlating with a difference in meaning (e.g. *cat bites dog* v. *dog bites cat*), or a change of ending (e.g. *dog* v. *dogs*). It is on this basis that it is possible to suggest several stages of grammatical development.[12]

---

[12] These stages are illustrated in detail in D. Crystal, P. Fletcher and M. Garman, *The grammatical analysis of language disability: a procedure for assessment and remediation* (Edward Arnold 1976). For a different conception of stages, see R. Brown, *A first language*. For a criticism of the current tendency to 'read in' grammar to early child utterances, see C. J. Howe, 'The meanings of two-word utterances in the speech of young children', *Journal of Child Language* 3 (1976), 29–47.

Stage I we have already encountered: the period from around 9 to 18 months where the majority of the sentences are single-element, e.g. *dada, there, no, gone, more*. It is not possible to say very much about the grammar of these sentences. We cannot say that *dada* is the 'subject' of an 'understood' sentence 'dada is there', as already argued, because of the impossibility of deciding this as against the claim that it is 'really' the 'object' of an understood sentence such as 'I see daddy.' Nor is it easy even to classify these words into parts of speech, as the *door* example above suggested (as well as the old problems of *allgone, gimme, ta, no*, cf. p. 31). We may classify their semantic or sociolinguistic function, possibly (see below), but not their grammar.

Stage II is from around 18 months until around 2, and contains the development of sentences that are 2 elements in length. There is, to begin with, a transitional stage, as sequences of single-element sentences come together, but lacking the prosodic coherence of a sentence where both elements are within the same intonational frame, e.g. **|**dada**|**gone**|** becomes **|**dada gone**|**. Typical sentences are: *dada there, more train, where mummy, gone car, my teddy*. It is difficult to describe these sentences precisely in grammatical terms, for similar reasons to those given in Stage I. Given a situation such as a child seeing his daddy kick a ball through a window, a Stage II child who knows the lexical items, *daddy, kick, ball* and *window* may come out with any pair, in any order, depending on which item he feels to be most salient, e.g. *daddy kick, daddy ball, ball window, window daddy*, etc. After a while, certain patterns will become more predictable than others (e.g. agent before action in English), but until this happens, it is not possible to be sure whether terms like *Subject, Verb, Object* are appropriate. Towards the beginning of Stage II, a child might say *tickle daddy* and mean either 'I'm going to tickle daddy' *or* 'I want daddy to tickle me.' If the context is clearly the latter, then we could say with confidence that the structure of the sentence is Verb-Subject; but the trouble is that often the context is not clear, and the sentence structure, in the absence of clear intonational or word-order clues, becomes indeterminate. By the end of Stage II the situation has usually improved, so that it becomes possible to see clear contextual or formal clues as to the sentence's meaning which would permit a confident grammatical analysis; some inflections have usually begun to emerge (e.g. *-ing, -s, -ed*), and word-order contrast is more stable. But as a general principle at Stage II, all grammatical analysis must proceed with caution.

Stage III runs from around 2 until around 2½, and shows the development of sentences containing three main elements, e.g. *daddy kick ball, that big bag, where man gone*. Some children will already have begun to 'fill out' some of these elements of sentence structure by attaching particles to the main words, e.g. *daddy kick a ball, daddy kicking ball*, but apart from noting that this process is a very gradual one, emerging in object position before subject position, there are few details available. Further inflectional endings emerge throughout this period, e.g. forms of the verb and noun, and the first uses of auxiliary verbs and pronouns appear. Utterances which contain the 'main' words of a sentence but lack the 'little', grammatical words and endings are sometimes called 'telegraphic'—but it should be clear from the above remarks that this could be a misleading label, if it is taken to mean that the child is 'leaving out' items he could have put in.

Stage IV continues the process begun in Stage III, increasing sentence structure so that it contains four or more main elements, e.g. *Susie going to town today, Where my mummy's hat gone, Steven give that to Lucy*. The point is no longer exactly how many elements each sentence contains: rather, a sentence may contain any number of elements up to the permitted maximum—in English, usually four or five. Parts of each element may not be fully developed (as in the examples just given), and children will be heard using grammatical words and endings with varying degrees of consistency, e.g. the *'s* sometimes being present, sometimes not. Noun phrases become more complex (e.g. *man with a hat on*), and this is particularly noticeable in post-verb positions in the sentence—in other words, commencing the process which makes the bulk of the length of a sentence in English appear after the verb rather than before. Another important development is the emergence of coordination within phrases (e.g. *boys and girls*). By the end of this stage, in short, the vast majority of the types of simple sentence (i.e sentences containing only one clause) have come to be used, viz. statements, questions, commands, transitive and intransitive clauses etc.[13] This presumably accounts for the widely voiced feeling that by 3, the child has learned the 'basic' grammar of his language.

There are however several things left to learn. *Stage V*, from around 3 to 3½, focuses on the learning of complex sentence structure (i.e. sentences containing more than one clause) and basic patterns of sentence sequence. The use of *and* to join clauses is particularly noticeable (*Daddy gone in the garden and—he felled over—and—and he hurt his knee . . .*), along with some other conjunctions, both coordinating and subordinating (e.g. *but, so, 'cos*). Clauses as objects are particularly common (e.g. *I said he did it*), and comparative structures (e.g. *it's bigger than that*) develop, along with the associated inflections. Phrases

---

[13] For an outline account, see Crystal, Fletcher and Garman, *The grammatical analysis of language disability*; for a detailed classification, see Quirk and Greenbaum, *A university grammar of English*.

also get more complex, with the emergence of relative clauses, etc. (e.g. *this is the house I built yesterday*).

By 3½, then, it can be said with some conviction that a child has learned the essential creativity of language: he can produce sentences that are indefinitely long, for once he has learned that a sentence can be made bigger by adding a clause on with *and*, he comes to repeat the process, often ad infinitum! He also has, as we have seen, a wide range of sentence types. 3½-year-old spontaneous speech is, therefore, rarely unintelligible. But it is still some way from adult speech, in two main respects. It contains a number of 'errors' (from the adult point of view), and a number of structures have still to be learned. It is important to keep the inverted commas around 'errors', because of course from the point of view of the child's developing system, they are not errors at all —on the contrary, they are signs of the child working out for himself the regularities and irregularities of the language (cf. p. 35). At 3½, at any rate, 'errors' are common, though they rarely impede intelligibility, e.g. *him going now, what you be doing?, you bettern't do that, nobody don't likes me*. The main thing that happens during the next year, which constitutes *Stage VI*, is that the various grammatical systems which are evidently still being developed come to be thoroughly acquired, e.g. the pronoun systems, the auxiliary verb system (at least as regards the way in which these forms are grammatically used— understanding the full meaning of *must, may, should* etc. takes several years longer). Most irregular verbs and nouns also come to be learned as such (though there are always some that seem to resist learning, often until well into primary school). In addition to this process of progressively eliminating syntactic or morphological error between 3½ and 4½, certain new grammatical features begin to develop. Passive structures emerge, e.g. *I just been stung by a wasp, I got kicked*, as do more complex ways of introducing noun phrases, e.g. *all/both/much/ many. . . .* It takes a long time before such structures come to be fully established (with passives, for instance, up to age 9 or 10), but their presence comes to be felt quite markedly at this Stage.

Stage VII deals with the acquisition of grammatical structure after age 4½. To some, it is surprising that such a Stage should exist at all. There is a view that by the time a child arrives at school, he can be assumed to have learned the grammar of his language. It is not the job of the teacher to teach basic grammatical patterns, it is argued: rather, the teacher's job is to provide the child with opportunities to use the grammar he has, and to extend its use into previously unfamiliar contexts. Now, without denying the importance of developing the child's functional awareness of language (see chapter 3), it is none the less the case that the primary assumption here is false. There is a great deal about the grammar of English speech that a child has *not* learned before he arrives at school, and the process of completing this knowledge of his language will continue until around puberty.

This remaining learning can be grouped under two headings, learning new structures, and learning to comprehend familiar structures fully. Under the first heading, there is the whole area of sentence connectivity, for example, over which the child has so far achieved only a limited command. Sentences are linked in many grammatical ways in English, e.g. the various types of adverbial connector, such as *actually, frankly, really, however*. It is not until around 7 that such items seem to become really widely used, e.g. *Actually I said I'd see him tonight*. The comment clauses referred to in chapter 1 (*you know* etc.) are also relatively late, as are variations in word order for emphasis, especially using constructions with *it* and *there* (e.g. *It was in the shop I said I'd see him, There were lots of people in the shop*).

The term 'comprehension', used above, is sometimes confusing. This does not refer to the technique of checking that the sense of a passage has been understood, but in the present context to the process of interpreting the structures of speech. It is a familiar point that children (and others) often use words they do not fully understand. What is less familiar is that this applies to syntax too. Here, it is often difficult to see that a mistake has been made, because the ambiguous sentence, as it stands, can be given a possible interpretation. A good example of the mismatch between production and comprehension occurs in the use of the passive voice. As we have seen, this comes to be well used before 5, but it would be misleading to assume that 5-year-olds can therefore handle all uses of the passive. Experiments involving the manipulation of toys show this not to be so. Give a child a dog and a cat and ask him to 'Show me "the dog bites the cat" ', and he will produce an appropriate response; but the request 'Show me "the dog is bitten by the cat" ' will be likely to produce an inappropriate response—the dog will be shown biting the cat again, as if the child had paid attention only to the salient lexical items (*dog-bite-cat*) and ignored the others. There are many constructions where similar problems appear (e.g. the use of certain subordinating conjunctions, such as *although, unless, since*), whose comprehension is relatively late. Some of the difficulties are increased due to semantic problems, e.g. the predictable confusion between *ask* and *tell*, where very similar meanings coincide in parallel structures (cf. *Ask daddy to come here* v. *Tell daddy to come here*).[14] Another example widely quoted is of the structure that became famous in outlines of generative grammar in the 1960s. The point of the two

[14] For this and the following example, see C. Chomsky, *The acquisition of syntax in children from five to ten* (MIT Press 1969). An example of the criticisms referred to below may be found in R. Cromer, 'Children are nice to understand: surface clues for the recovery of a deep structure', *British Journal of Psychology* 61 (1970), 397–408.

sentences, *John is eager to please* and *John is easy to please*, is to show that sentences may appear identical but in fact display fundamental differences. On the surface, the two sentences are the same: the subject in both cases is *John*, the verb is *is*, and the complement consists of an adjective followed by an infinitive phrase. But as adult speakers of the language, we know that the two sentences do not mean the same. In the first sentence, *John is eager to please*, it is John who wishes to please some other, unspecified person. He is performing the action. But in the second sentence, he is *being pleased* by some unspecified person. He is receiving the action. Putting it into syntactic terms, he is the underlying subject of the first sentence, but the underlying object of the second. Now *we* know this: the question is, when do children come to appreciate this distinction? What Carol Chomsky did was to present a group of children, aged from five upwards, with a blindfolded doll, and ask them 'Is this doll easy to see or hard to see?' If the children said 'Easy to see' then it is argued that they have learned the distinction; but if they said 'Hard to see', and amplified their comment (upon request) by for instance, 'Because it's got a blindfold on', then it is argued that they had not learned it. The Chomsky results showed that before the age of six this distinction was hardly ever learned, whereas after seven it was known to nearly *all* children in the sample. Now while aspects of Chomsky's methodology have been questioned, it is possible to extract a general conclusion from this and similar experiments, namely, that there are matters of structural (and in this case also semantic) interpretation which it takes children many years to acquire.

In short, what the child has to learn after age 5 is that there are layers in the interpretation of a sentence that are not immediately apparent from perceiving the form of the sentence. Sentences do not always mean what they seem to mean. And it is worth noting that it is only when this process starts that children begin to appreciate the various effects it is possible to introduce into language using it—for example, jokes, riddles, puns, and the like, which rely for their effect on the detection of ambiguity.

When does the learning of grammar come to an end, therefore? 'Puberty' has been mentioned, and there is some evidence to suggest that at or around puberty, the nature of the language-learning process in man alters radically. There is some evidence of differential ability to learn foreign languages pre- and post-puberty, but this is rather indirect (in view of the difficulty of controlling such variables as motivation); also, the evidence of stylistic comparison of ranges of structures used in spontaneous speech in the two periods (showing that pre-puberty speech is more homogeneous, while post-puberty displays greater idiosyncrasy and inventiveness) is limited. Rather more specific is the evidence from language pathology, where certain types of abnormality respond very differently to exposure to language and therapy before and after puberty.[15] Perhaps the question at the head of this paragraph is an unnecessary one. Certainly, in contrast with vocabulary and style (which never stop developing), it must be pointed out that the learning of phonology and grammar is a finite process; but there is little empirical support as yet relating to the linguistic analysis of the 'middle years'.

Throughout this section I have talked about general stages of syntactic development. Before moving to a different topic, it is worth illustrating the way in which specific syntactic themes can be traced developmentally in this way. A good example of stable order of development comes from the detailed work on the acquisition of questions carried out by Ursula Bellugi and others.[16] But as always in work on language acquisition, we must begin with a specification of the goal: what range of questions *are* there to be acquired in English—that is, in the adult language? Basically, there are four, and they are as follows. Questions may be formed, firstly, by inverting the order of subject and verb: *You are coming* becomes *Are you coming?* Secondly, questions may be formed by adding a question-word at the beginning of the sentence—a word such as *What, How, Where, When* . . . For example, *You are coming* becomes *When are you coming?*—and we should notice here that not only is a question-word introduced, but the order of subject and verb changes as well. Thirdly, we may add a tag-question to the sentence—for instance, *isn't it? aren't they? You're coming, aren't you?* with a rising intonation. And lastly, we may add a questioning attitude to a statement, by using a rising intonation: *You're coming?* How is this adult system acquired?

There does seem to be a regular order. First comes the questioning attitude using intonation. By 12 months the child can make the distinction between identifying and questioning, using intonation, e.g. *Dada?* as opposed to *Dada!* At around 18 months the first syntactic questions are heard, and these involve the use of a question-word, especially *Where* or *What*—for example, *What that? Where dada?* What seems to be happening here is that the child is simply adding his question-word to sentences he was previously producing. He takes a sentence, and if he wants to turn it into a question, he attaches the question-word to it—sometimes at the end, but usually at the beginning. This strategy remains for quite a time, even though his sentence patterns increase in complexity. The 2-year-old who is beginning to produce quite complex 3-element sentences (such as *Teddy be hiding*) will question these sentences still by simply adding the question-word—for example, *Where teddy be hiding?* He has not yet learned to alter the order of the

[15] See E. Lenneberg, *The biological foundations of language* (New York, Wiley 1967), esp. 142 ff.

[16] E. S. Klima and U. Bellugi, 'Syntactic regularities in the speech of children', in J. Lyons and R. Wales (eds.), *Psycholinguistics papers* (Edinburgh University Press 1966), 183–213.

subject and the verb within the sentence. Making the inversion in fact only takes place *after* the general idea of using Verb-Subject ordering to ask questions has been acquired, and this is a separate process. For it is well into the third year that questions such as *Are you coming?* begin to emerge in the child's production; and it is only *after* this that the inversion will be used in the question-word questions as well. Thus at 2½, we might hear a child using both *Are you coming?* and *Where you are coming?* On the face of it, this seems quite chaotic—until we realize that separate processes of acquisition are involved. Tag-questions, finally, come to be systematically used last of all.

Semantics
In view of the importance of meaning in the study of language, it may perhaps seem paradoxical that semantic development in children has received far less attention than either grammar or phonology. But it should not be surprising when we remember the difficulties inherent in making any study of meaning at all.[17] At least with phonology and grammar, there are tangible features of language form to look out for. Meaning, however, arises from the way in which forms are used in relation to the extralinguistic world of objects, ideas and experiences. It cannot be seen, or measured, in any simple way. And with young children, there is the additional complexity that, unlike adults, we cannot ask them directly what a word or sentence 'means'. Only careful studies of taperecording and videotape are likely to establish patterns of semantic function and development, and it is only recently that the methodological problems involved in obtaining naturalistic samples of data have begun to be overcome.

All that can be done in this section is to illustrate some of the kinds of semantic development characteristic of various periods, and to point to the difficulties in using the commonest traditional measure of semantic development—vocabulary growth. The problems in using this measure are easily illustrated by the disagreement between textbooks as to how many words the average child of a particular age is likely to have. Estimates range from 2000 words, for a 5-year-old, to 10,000. Some of the problems are: Are we counting active vocabulary (i.e. words that the child actually uses) or passive vocabulary (i.e. words he understands, but does not use)? If the latter, there are going to be difficulties in deciding whether a word used to a child by a parent or teacher is understood or not. If the former, there are going to be difficulties in deciding how often a child needs to have used a word before we can say he has learned it. The first occasion of use might be quite inappropriate, or might represent a guess on the child's part as to the use of the word. Would we then only include as part of a child's

---

[17] See Palmer, *Semantics*.

active vocabulary those words that are heard to be used more than once; and if so, how often? Different writers on semantic development make different decisions.

Another problem is deciding how words are to be identified. Are *it's, won't* etc. to be counted as one word or two? Are idiomatic constructions to be counted as single items, even though they may contain many words (e.g. *cats and dogs* in *it's raining cats and dogs*—cf. p. 31)? Are learned phrases, such as *A stitch in time saves nine*, to be counted as separate words? There are many difficulties of this kind. Then there is the question of meaning. Some lexical items have many senses (they are *polysemic*). Common verbs, like *take, come, see*, may have up to 20 or 30 uses. If the child uses the verb *see*, then it is not the case that he has learned that verb in its semantic entirety. Rather he has learned a particular sense of the verb. And the same applies to the vast majority of common words in English: they are polysemic, as a glance at any dictionary will show, and they will therefore be acquired sense by sense. Rather than count vocabulary, then, it would be more realistic to count senses. Putting it another way, if two children could be shown to have a vocabulary of 50 and 100 words respectively, the traditional approach would say that the second child was more advanced. But if the 50-word child was using each of his words in various different ways, producing more than one sense for each word, while the 100-word child was not, it would be very doubtful to suggest that he was in fact ahead, from a semantic point of view. This is only a hypothetical case, but in practice problems of this sort turn up all the time. The number of different words used, then, is only one factor in the study of semantic development. It is the *sense* of a word which matters, and we have already seen some of the problems involved in identifying (and thus counting) senses, especially in the early period (cf. p. 40).

Even if we do succeed in counting vocabulary items, however, we will have learned little of semantic development. A far more important issue is to determine whether there are certain kinds of meaning that emerge earliest in child language, and how the building up of the semantic structure of the language proceeds from there. Certain major tendencies have begun to be systematically studied, and as a consequence over-simple ideas about the learning of meaning have come to be soundly criticized. The view that a child learns the meaning of a word 'all at once', alluded to above, is patently false, for instance, as is the idea that he builds up his vocabulary 'a word at a time'. The first of these views can be attacked on the evidence of the many 'over-extended' meanings of early words, some of which have already been illustrated. Early vocabulary is characterized by the child using a word on the basis of a partial awareness of its meaning, e.g. *dog* is something which barks, or something with four legs—on the basis of which, *anything* which barks, or has four legs, is likely to be labelled *dog* for a while, until the child begins to see distinguishing features (between *dog* and *cat*, *dog* and *horse* etc.). Good examples of semantic progression up to about 2½ years are given in Eve Clark's writing; for example, she cites a 1920 study where the word *bebe* was first used by the child to refer to his reflections in a mirror, then to a photograph of himself, then to all photographs, then to all pictures, then tô all books with pictures, and finally to all books. It would be impossible to explain why that child called a book a 'baby' without a detailed knowledge of this etymology.[18]

Children will of course vary enormously in the way they extend (or fail to extend) the meaning of words, but it does seem to be the case that the earliest features of meaning used in the identification of words are based on the primary perceptions of movement, shape, size, sound, taste and texture (especially the first four). There are several unresolved issues about this process (e.g. whether the child uses these percepts first to construct very abstract or very specific senses), but certain tendencies arising from this view now seem clear. One principle which follows from it is that the semantic features that are more general or more central to the meaning of a word will be acquired first. For example, children first learn that *brother* is 'male' and 'not adult'; later, that *brother* implies 'more than one in the same generation'; and later still, that if a boy *has* a brother, then he *is* a brother (the 'reciprocal' aspect of the definition). Most of the central kinship terms are fully comprehended by age 10, but the secondary terms (e.g. *cousin, nephew*) are still far from complete, because they involve more semantic features, and are thus more complex.

The view that vocabulary is learned 'a word at a time' is also false. Words are always used in contexts, and therefore the meaning of a word will be partly dependent on the other words which accompany it in a sentence, as well as those with which it is in contrast at any point within the sentence. Looking at words in sequence first, an item such as *table* is unclear in the following incomplete sentence:

That's a fine table

Adding the phrase *and chairs* provides one interpretation; adding *of figures* provides another. Part of the task of understanding the use of the word *table*, therefore, is to see the sort of word it goes with ('collocates with' is the usual technical term). Children have to learn the collocation of words, and can be seen doing so as they make mistakes in their use (e.g. *loaf of cake, drive a bicycle, the fire is sore*). Later, they have to learn that some collocations are fixed, i.e. idiomatic. This is a fairly late process, as illustrated by the 7-year-old who returned

[18] E. Clark, 'What's in a word? On the child's acquisition of semantics in his first language', in T. E. Moore (ed.), *Cognitive development and the acquisition of language* (New York, Academic Press 1973).

home most concerned about his headmaster's larder—the man having said he 'hadn't got a sausage'. Also a late process is the learning of specific ways of comparing lexical items, using figures of speech: early attempts at completing similes produce examples like *It was as big as big*, or . . . *big as anything*; later stages involve the use of literal comparison (e.g. . . . *big as a mountain*); later still, use is made of less obvious analogies (e.g. . . . *big as a disc-jockey's smile*)—these last examples not emerging until well into a child's teens.[19]

Looking at words in contrast involves seeing the possibilities of substitution at any point within a sentence, e.g.

The big table was in the garden.
A small chair was in the garden.
That round ball was in the garden.

It is clear that many of the substitute words 'go together', in the sense that they define each other in various ways, e.g. *big* is the opposite of *small*, *table* and *chair* can both be grouped under the more general terms *furniture*. These synonyms, antonyms, and other relations of meaning are also part of the overall use of a word in a language. We have to learn the words that can stand in for each other without major change of meaning, the words that are opposite, the words that can summarize, and so on. And there is evidence to show that children do try out words in different ways to ascertain their range of applicability, e.g. the following 2-year-old's paraphrasing sequence:

That not broken—it fixed now—no break it any more. . . .

Another example is with adjective sets: to begin with, all water may be *hot*; then *hot* may be opposed to *cold*; then when *cool* and *warm* come to be used, they affect the meaning of the other words, delimiting them further. This process of integrating new words within vocabulary that is already known—the new word 'elbowing its way in' as it were, and causing redefinition of the other words in the process—is not particularly suprising, of course, as it is also a common means of learning new vocabulary for adults also. The important point is that this 'simultaneous' learning of the meanings of words starts very early, well within the second year of life. Presenting lexical contrasts is also one of the main strategies used by the parent to the child—as it is, indeed, later on by the teacher to the pupil.

Sociolinguistics

Under the heading of 'sociolinguistic development', various kinds of information could be listed, e.g. the way in which the child develops his individual and group sense of language (his dialect, in particular),

[19] See H. Gardner, M. Kircher, E. Winner and D. Perkins, 'Children's metaphoric productions and preferences', *Journal of Child Language* 2 (1975), 125–41.

both in terms of his own use of language and his recognition of variation in the language of others. It is possible to see variations in the child's first-year vocalizations, for instance, that seem to anticipate the role-playing of later life. At 12 months, one child was recorded playing in his cot with his small rabbit and large panda. The vocalization was entirely babble, but when the child 'acted' the rabbit responding to him, he put on a falsetto voice, and when he 'acted 'the panda respond-ing, he put on a deep, 'chesty' voice. From around a year, it is possible to see children consciously 'playing' with language, making various phonetic and other effects. Between 2 and 3 there are clear signs of their developing linguistic strategies to gain their intentions, e.g. using a focusing remark to prepare someone else for action:

> X. You see that train? Y. Yes. X. Well, I want it.[20]

They also try out various linguistic strategies on parents too, e.g. to see how far they can pursue a line of inquiry before sanctions are imposed. An example described by Piaget is the repetitive use of *Why*-questions, where a causal sense is obviously not intended (the child often knows the answer to the question he asks), and where the function of the interchange seems more to do with the child 'learning how to ask'.[21] By 3, stylistic variations are commonly heard in role-play: playing at being daddy means using certain features of daddy-language, for example. It is also between 2 and 3 that parents first begin to introduce explicitly and more systematically stylistic comments, such as 'Don't shout at table', 'Say please', or 'Don't talk like that to the vicar'!

Another aspect of sociolinguistics is the way in which the interaction between parent and child develops and changes as the child grows older. In the first year, there are several interaction patterns, some so subtle that they have only recently come to be discovered by the meticulous analysis of videotape, e.g. the patterns of eye contact between mother and child. Some of the vocalization patterns are highly complex also, and have been characterized as 'protoconversa-tions', as when the mother responds to the child's noises, aping them and making a fuss over them. Far from babies copying their parents' noises in the first year, it seems that more often the parents imitate the children, producing the range of baby-talk that acts as a marker of intimacy between parent and child. A further basic point about the first year is the way in which several of these linguistic interactions are bound up with nonlinguistic factors. As Jerome Bruner has stressed, certain uses of language cannot be explained without referring to the

[20] See C. Garvey, 'Requests and responses in children's speech', *Journal of Child Language* 2 (1975), 41–63.
[21] J. Piaget, *The language and thought of the child* (3rd edition, Routledge and Kegan Paul 1959), 164 ff.

general pattern of activity of which they form an essential part.[22] The action pattern would be meaningless without the language, and the language meaningless without the action pattern. Good examples are games like 'peep-bo': to hide behind a towel, regularly peeping out, is predictably accompanied by some linguistic climax, such as 'boo', which alternates with the visual activity. Both factors, linguistic and nonlinguistic, are essential for an appreciation of the effect.

In the second year, the linguistic strategies of interaction used by the parent develop in several ways. One of the best-studied is the way in which the parent unconsciously expands the utterances of the child so as to turn them into 'full' sentences, e.g. *daddy gone* may be responded to by *Yes, daddy's gone*. There is some evidence that children responded to in this way make more progress in language than children whose parents do not expand their utterances. Likewise, there is evidence that if expansion is further developed by *paraphrase*, i.e. making the same or a similar point in a different way, progress is still further facilitated, e.g. 'Yes, daddy's gone. He's gone to work, in his big car'.[23] During the third year, the parents' use of questions develops in ways quite unlike adult speech, e.g.

Child   Want car.
Adult   You want a car? This one? Or that one?
Child   That blue one.
Adult   The blue one! That *is* a nice colour, isn't it? . . .

Such 'echo' questions and comments serve the important function of clarifying the child's speech for him, thus permitting the parent to arrive at a satisfactory interpretation of language that is often ambiguous, because of its limited vocabulary and syntax. The adult has to keep checking—not only that he has understood the child's intentions, but that the child has understood his. (At this stage, it should be noted, child speech lacks the response cues that would normally signal continued understanding in adult interactions, e.g. *mhm, yeah*: cf. p. 24.)

By making explicit the assumptions and implications underlying what the child is saying, the parent's questioning strategy can also be interpreted as a teaching method—showing the child how to speak. This process becomes very important in the fourth year, where the redundancy of parental speech becomes even more marked. The parent

[22] J. Bruner, 'The ontogenesis of speech acts', *Journal of Child Language* 2 (1975), 1–19.
[23] For expansion, see R. Brown and U. Bellugi, 'Three processes in the child's acquisition of syntax', in E. H. Lenneberg (ed.), *New directions in the study of language* (MIT Press 1964), 131–61. On expansion and paraphrase, see K. E. Nelson, G. Carskaddon and J. D. Bonvillian, 'Syntax acquisition: impact of experimental variation in adult verbal interaction with the child', *Child Development* 44 (1973) 497–504.

continues to provide extra context, often without giving the child a chance to reply to an initial sentence (e.g. *Where's teddy? Is he outside?*) Exaggerated responses are common (e.g. *That's a clever boy*). But there is an important difference from earlier attempts to 'socialize' the child using language: the parent now starts introducing some assumptions of his own. Certain things come gradually to be taken for granted. For example, there is the use of the 'hidden imperative', e.g. *Would you like to shut the door?*—where the question form hides a command function. Initially, the child will treat that as a question, and answer *yes* or *no*. (By the time he reaches school, however, it will be in his best interests to have learned that the answer *no* will not be appreciated.) A similar hidden function can be attributed to statements also, as in school dialogues such as:

T   That tube's broken.
Child Yes, sir.
T   Don't just say yes sir. I want to know who did it.

Children have to learn to 'read between the lines' in such cases—to perceive the intention beneath the form (to interpret the nature of the 'speech act', as current terminology puts it). Normally, children will have had plenty of practice in reading between the lines, with parents introducing such subtleties into their speech from the third year. For children whose home background has lacked this kind of dialogue, though, there may well be a genuine lack of comprehension when faced in school with statements that do not state, or questions that do not ask.

A good example of the adult assumptions that come to be introduced into parent–child interaction at around 4 years of age is the way in which parents say 'no'. The straight negative response is the norm in earlier years, but it gradually gets replaced by 'reasoned' responses, such as:

(*Can I have a biscuit?*)	*After tea.*
	Ask daddy.
(*Can I go out now?*)	*It's raining.*
	Why not play with your train?
(*I want to turn this*)	*It won't work if you do.*
	I'll smack you.
	Very slowly then.
(*I want to climb on the table*)	*Big boys don't climb on tables.*
	You'll hurt yourself.

The logical gap between child sentence and adult response in these sequences is sometimes extremely wide, but somehow most children manage to bridge it. How they do so is still unclear. But at least the magnitude of the task can be appreciated, and thus in cases of remedial language work, the over-use of such assumptions avoided (see further chapter 3).[24]

Once at school, the nature of the child's sociolinguistic experience changes radically. For the first time, he will be systematically exposed to new dialects and accents; he will be faced with the linguistic demands of relatively formal social situations, and he will have to deduce the rules of learning from language that may often be opaque. The problems of developing teaching strategies that match the linguistic abilities and expectations of the child now need to be faced, therefore, and these are discussed in detail in the next chapter.

*

The treatment of child language acquisition in this chapter is by no means comprehensive. Moreover, it has not dealt with questions of major theoretical importance, such as the relationship of comprehension to production, the relationship of learning strategies (such as imitation) to linguistic progress, the relationship between development and acquisition, or the variations in the rate of learning that relate to such factors as socioeconomic background. The contemporary research emphasis on the nature of mother–child interaction has also only been hinted at. But even from just a few examples it should be possible to draw several conclusions. In particular, it should be clear that the idea of simple 'scores' of language development is unlikely to be possible. *Quantitative* indices, if they are to be of value, will have to be complex things, containing many variables. Personally, I prefer to work with *qualitative* pictures, or 'profiles' of development—systematic presentations of the sounds, structures, semantic features, or whatever, that can be established in a sample of child usage. The number of instances of the features found in the sample is calculated, but no attempt is made to 'collapse' all these figures into a single total that might be claimed to represent a 'development level'. An example of a profile for grammar is given on p. 91. Such models are still very tentative, and unstandardized, but they can none the less have considerable practical usefulness in helping to organize observations about a child's language behaviour.

Despite these gaps and limitations, it should be clear from this chapter that a great deal of progress has been made in understanding child language acquisition. The field is still in its infancy, but already

---

[24] The negation example is illustrated further, along with others, in F. F. Schachter, D. Fosha, S. Stemp, N. Brotman and S. Ganger, 'Everyday caretaker talk to toddlers v. threes and fours', *Journal of Child Language* 3 (1976), 221–45. On other linguistic aspects of socialization, mother language etc., see C. Snow, 'Mothers' speech to children learning language', *Child Development* 43 (1972), 549–65; J. B. Gleason, 'Code-switching in children's language', in Moore (ed.), *Cognitive development and the acquisition of language*.

several of the misleading assumptions of traditional study have been successfully challenged, a number of facts about development have been accumulated, and several hypotheses about the processes under-lying acquisition advanced. We are a long way from any comprehensive theoretical explanation of language acquisition, but there is plenty of information which seems able to be put to immediate practical use in the construction and evaluation of language-teaching procedures. How, then, might this be done?

Chapter 3   Language learning

Despite a certain impression to the contrary, there is no such thing as a linguistic 'approach' to the study of language-learning skills (whether speaking, listening, reading or writing), in the sense of a specific technique derived wholly from the theories, methods and empirical findings of general linguistics. The role of linguistics, I have argued, is more general and also more fundamental than this: it is to inculcate a state of mind, to provide a set of principles which can shape professional attitudes towards specific problems, and which, because they come from a coherent scientific framework, can inspire confidence when it comes to suggesting solutions. Putting this another way, the aim is to develop explicitly-principled teaching or therapeutic procedures. We need to be consciously aware of what we are doing with language, and why, and be able to explain our position to others, so that rational discussion about strengths and weaknesses can proceed. I now propose to discuss in more detail some of the relevant linguistic principles that can help to underpin pedagogic practice; also the kinds of problem that have hindered the implementation of these principles, and the kinds of strategy that seem to be effective. These principles emerge at so many points that it is not possible to be comprehensive. I shall accordingly select two main areas by way of illustration, rather summarily labelling them as the principle of 'expectancy' and the principle of 'appropriateness', before proceeding to a general discussion of the possibility of an integrated approach to problems of mother-tongue language learning.[1]

The principle of expectancy
It now seems to be axiomatic that the language presented to children in the classroom should as far as possible be compatible with the *expectations* of the child. A succinct statement is to be found in the Bullock Report:

---

[1] For a general discussion of this field, see C. B. Cazden, *Child language and education* (Holt, Rinehart and Winston 1972); C. B. Cazden, V. P. John and D. Hymes (eds.), *Functions of language in the classroom* (New York, Teachers College Press 1972); and other references below.

a printed text is easier to read the more closely its structures are related to those used by the reader in normal speech. . . . Reading material which presents children with . . . unreal language therefore lacks predictability and prevents them from making use of the sequential probability in linguistic structure. . . . (92)

Unless there is a close match between the syntactic features of the text and the syntactic expectancies of the reader there will be a brake on the development of word identification. . . . (105)

It is a point that has often been made in other terms—for example, insisting that language materials must be 'relevant' or 'familiar'—but the implications of this principle have been less widely recognized, and the difficulties in implementing it are still not fully anticipated. It is easy to criticize materials which go against this principle, but less easy to see what kinds of material might be put in their place, and how we can be confident that the child's expectations are in fact being met.

Criticism of well-established materials is a task that is often misunderstood as simply poking fun; but it is a necessary stage of progress, and it can be highly instructive. The contemporary focus of attention here is on grammar, which, in the context of the study of reading and language-development skills, has been the most neglected level of language structure. Plenty of time has been spent on such matters as vocabulary enrichment (keywords, antonyms, figures of speech etc.) and the relationship between pronunciation and spelling (the discussion of the relative merits of phonic- or word-based approaches); but grammar has received next to no systematic study. Yet as we have seen (p. 28), grammar is the central organizing principle or structuring process in language, without which sounds, no matter how well spelled, and words, no matter how well recognized, remain isolated units, a disorganized juxtaposition of noises and ideas. Grammar relates sound to sense, and provides the most direct measure of developing linguistic ability. For the teacher of early language, then, and of reading in particular, it would seem essential (a) to be aware of the level of grammatical ability attained by a child in order to see whether the grammar of the materials being presented is within the child's capabilities, and (b) to be able to criticize the grammatical standards of materials on such grounds as realism, familiarity, and gradability.

It is not difficult to find examples of alien or unfamiliar grammatical structures in the traditional reading schemes. *What have you in the shop?* is a pattern no longer in general use (though it was common enough in Elizabethan English—'What have you there, sirrah?'). *One little kitten runs to the basket* is strange in two respects: the initial *one* is awkward (unless it is intended to make a contrast using intonation—*one* kitten runs, *others* stay behind—which is not the normal classroom interpretation), and the simple present tense form is unreal—unless a sports commentary context is understood! A third example is *A small red jug stood next*. And there are many more which in isolation may seem trivial, but put together produce an artificial kind of English syntax which is far removed from anything that a child might be said to 'expect' on the basis of his earlier language experience. There is nothing particularly odd about a few present tenses; but when entire series are placed in the present tense, one begins to wonder. Or again, there is nothing exceptional about *I see a book and a pen* and *I see a table and a desk*; but when the material develops into *A book and a pen are on a table and a desk*, and so on, the impact of the artificiality is more worrying.

To implement point (a) above, and thus avoid these criticisms, requires the use of some kind of yardstick for assessing linguistic progress. I have argued elsewhere that the only feasible yardstick available at present is that provided by the studies of normal language acquisition, reviewed in chapter 2 above.[2] It would be very nice if we had available independent measures of complexity of sentence structure—so that we could prove that one sentence was simpler than another, and therefore should be introduced first in any teaching programme. But no such measures of complexity exist, and the suggestions that have been made are highly controversial. We can see this by trying to decide whether two sentences are equivalent or different in complexity. It is easy enough with sentences such as *The cat sat on the mat*, which is undeniably less complex than *People who smoke will be criticized*, but how sure could we be about *The man in the corner saw the cat* as opposed to *The man saw the cat in the corner?* Are they the same, or is one more complex than the other, and if so, which? It is possible to order these with respect to when they would normally emerge in the speech of young children (the second usually appearing before the first, in fact), but it does not follow from this that the second is necessarily more complex than the first, in all circumstances. Too many variables enter into the notion of complexity (such as attention, motivation, and the preceding linguistic context) to enable it to be used as a simple yardstick for assessing progress or grading structures. The stages of development outlined in chapter 2, however, despite their inadequacies and gaps, are more reliable as an index of progress. Using a developmental ordering of that general kind—and remembering to pay attention to the detail as well as to the outline of development—it is possible to 'place' a child in terms of his syntactic development, and decide how far above or behind his group he may happen to be. It is then a feasible—though complex—pedagogic task to find reading materials or language-development materials which do not overtax his syntactic ability by

[2] See Crystal, Fletcher and Garman, *The grammatical analysis of language disability*, chapter 2.

making him read or use structures which he has not yet learned in speech. (Any of the points raised in Stage VII above (p. 47) would presumably be out of place in the early books of a reading scheme, for instance.) After the child has mastered the basic skills of reading, of course, then that medium can be used as a means of extending and experimenting with syntax, and developing a child's linguistic ability in general. But in the early months of reading, it would seem pedagogically unsound to attempt to introduce the reading skill if there is going to be persistent interference from unfamiliar syntax. The point is usually accepted as obvious with vocabulary, but it applies to other levels of language structure besides.

The simple idea underlying the sentence-maker in *Breakthrough to Literacy* was one main reason why that scheme was a breakthrough. The child now had available a device which enabled him to see precisely those syntactic patterns which he wanted to express, and which were therefore likely to be part of his normal language background. Indeed, some of the spontaneous sentences produced on the sentence-maker by children experimenting with their new-found abilities in word recognition are a close reflection of the early patterns of sentence development noted in speech in chapter 2, e.g. *see daddy* put on the frame first, by a child who had said that she was going to 'write' *I want to see daddy*. But the sentence-maker, by itself, is no reading scheme; and when one moves on to consider the properties of reading schemes as wholes, a further cautionary point must be made. The principle of expectancy does not require that the materials used in a reading scheme (or indeed in the samples of speech usage that might constitute a general language-development programme) should *reflect* the norms of everyday, spontaneous, informal colloquial English, i.e. the kind of language illustrated in chapter 1, which is what most children are most used to before they arrive in school. On the contrary, for the written language to reflect the spoken language would be to deny the autonomy of each, the fact that each has an independent purpose that it is essential to maintain (see further below). It is almost as unreal a desideratum as one which tried to produce materials that bore *no* relation to speech at all. Apart from the fact that it is impossible for the written language to reflect speech in its entirety (the intonation system is an obvious discrepancy), there is also the point that no one would ever really want it to do so (bearing in mind the use of loose structuring, elliptical sentences, and so on). The term 'reflect' is misleading. A better term is 'compatible'; the structures of the written language ought to be compatible with those of the child's speech ability, i.e. not go beyond them in too marked a way, being neither too simple nor too advanced for the level of language development the child happens to be at. If the structures are compatible, then the principle of expectancy is being applied.

To be confident that the language we use in materials matches the patterns the children have used previously is an essential step in developing a principled teaching policy. But it is not the only step. We have still to ensure that the child is in fact making the match, and identifying the visual structure with his auditory structure. If a child is presented with the structure, *Ducks can swim*, then the fact that there is evidence from language-acquisition studies that he has used this structure previously is no guarantee that the spoken form of this sentence and its written form will be matched in the child's brain. Indeed, many of the 'comprehension' errors of daily classroom experience suggest that often the child does *not* make such a match: he may be able to read a structure aloud, but unable to relate it to the corresponding structure in speech (especially if read in a 'word at a time' intonation and rhythm); or he may write a spoken structure in an unexpected way, showing he has mis-analysed it (e.g. writing 'The buses are coming' as 'The bus is are coming'). How, then, can we ensure that spoken and written syntax will be related?

One possibility would be to focus explicitly on the structure at issue, by forcing the child to bridge the gap himself. This is one of the aims of *Skylarks*, for example.[3] In booklet 1 of that series, each page is devoted to a single sentence, as follows:

A fish can swim.	Frogs swim and jump.
A grasshopper can jump.	Most birds can fly.
Squirrels can climb trees.	A monkey jumps and climbs.
Ducks swim and fly.	

So far, apart from the selection of that particular structure, and the drill emphasis, there is little to differentiate this from many other approaches. The difference comes on the final page, where the sentences run:

Can you jump?   Can you swim?   Can you climb?   Can you fly?

Now, if the child is going to respond at all, either spontaneously or following example, the responses are likely to be 'Yes I can', 'I can't swim', and the like. In other words, the child has been led to use in his speech precisely the structures that he has seen being used immediately previously. There is thus a greater chance of a bridge between speech and reading being built than if he were responding in an unstructured way. The use of questions and commands are convenient ways of introducing this linguistic involvement on the part of the child. There is also the additional implication that this may be one way of establishing a more controlled reinforcement between the efforts of teacher and parent. The reaction of a parent to a child's reader may be very different from that of his teacher using the same book. There may be differences

    [3] J. Bevington and D. Crystal, *Skylarks* (London, Nelson 1975).

of emphasis, timing, interpretation, and other things. Given some way of predicting linguistic response, such as that illustrated above, there is a correspondingly greater chance of the parent's and the teacher's responses being in parallel, instead of in conflict. This, at least, is the hope. It is however a claim in need of empirical support, which can only come when detailed studies of teacher–parent integration come to be made.

Establishing a formal correspondence between the structures of speech and those of writing immediately brings us into contact with the problem of punctuation. This is another topic that tends to be minimized, perhaps in reaction to days when punctuation was taught with a ferocity almost unequalled in English teaching. But the pendulum swing which makes some teachers pay no attention to it at all, on the grounds that children will 'pick it up' in due course, is a retrograde emphasis. Children may, over a long period, 'pick up' some punctuation, but it is likely to be inaccurate in several respects, and in the interim, several additional difficulties will have emerged for the analysis and comprehension of sentence structures. We can see this in the kinds of error made in reading aloud by children who have not had any principles of sentence demarcation introduced to them. A frequent error is due to the mismatch between grammatical and line boundaries, which unless anticipated, causes inevitable problems. Layouts such as

They went for a ride
on a pony. The next day . . .

will be predictably read as

'They 'went 'for 'a 'ride/ –
'On 'a 'pony 'the 'next 'day . . .

with the main emphasis in line 1 on *ride*, followed by a pause. The error may be interpreted by the teacher as one of comprehension, and it may have repercussions which permeate several lines; but basically the difficulty arises out of formal linguistic considerations, and is not essentially a problem of comprehension at all. At the end of the first line, the child has to do one of the most difficult reading tasks of all, namely, find the beginning of the next line. While his eyes move, there is a pause, and the pitch of the voice will tend to fall. The first line's syntax is also a possible complete sentence in English, and so it is not surprising if the reader assumes that the sentence has come to an end, and treats the second line as a new sentence, with raised pitch and new prominence. The whole of the second line will then be read as the beginning of a single new sentence, unless the child's attention has previously been drawn to the two graphic phenomena which show that it is not, namely the full stop and the capital letter. If awareness of these is not present, there is little chance of any self-correction taking place until farther down the page.

This is no isolated example. Another very common error is in cases like:

'I want to go,' Janet said. 'I will come too,' said John.

The predictable difficulty is that the child will tend to pause after *go*, and then treat *Janet said* as going with the next sentence. *Said John* is then left in the air, or linked with the following sentence—and so the error grows. Once again, it is the mismatch between intonation and punctuation, induced through a lack of awareness of the latter, which causes the difficulty.

I am suggesting, then, that punctuation (and associated features such as spacing and layout) becomes less of a problem if it can be related systematically to the intonation system of the language, which is the main means the child has previously had of delimiting and linking grammatical structures. Simple, single-line sentences can be shown to be speakable using a single intonation/rhythm unit, the teacher providing a counterpoint of intonationally coherent sentences to the word-by-word intonations produced by the child. In this way the child begins to sense the structural function of pitch and pause, and this can provide a basis for introducing the main marks of punctuation, especially the capital letter and full stop. No sophisticated knowledge of intonation is necessary for this—simply an awareness on the part of the teacher that the process is systematic and gradable.

A further example of the importance of intonation lies in its role in making sentence patterns acceptable which would otherwise not be so, due to the reading materials (consciously or unconsciously) including deviant or rare sentence structures. A classic example is:

One little,
Two little,
Three little kittens.

The comma plus capital punctuation indicates that this cannot be read as prose. Unless read with an appropriate 'bouncing' nursery-rhyme intonation and rhythm, it produces an impossible grammatical structure for English:

One / little / two / little / three / little / kittens /.

Apart from this, it could lay the seeds of some very strange ideas as to when capital letters may be used. And there are many such cases, which need a specific intonation pattern to be meaningful. Try reading these with the emphasis solely on the last word, for example:

He saw toys and toys and toys.
I can eat caps (said the goat). I shall eat caps.
May I have a coat, a little coat for my doll?

All the examples so far have been of formal structures that raise problems for implementing the principle of expectancy. But this principle raises interesting questions in another area of linguistic analysis too, that of function. Expectancy here means that the *variety* of language being presented to the child in speech or writing should show some correspondence with that he is used to. The point has often been made in relation to the discussion of linguistic disadvantage, but it is more fundamental than this, as it affects all children in varying degrees. A familiar issue is the way in which the selection of vocabulary in a reading scheme needs to be thought of in relation to the child's previous socioeconomic or educational background—whether it should be 'Mother' (*Janet and John*) or 'Mum' (*Breakthrough to Literacy*) or 'Mummy', for example. This is not so much a linguistic issue as one for the sociologist and psychologist to contribute to. But there are none the less linguistic issues, when these more general matters have been taken into account. To begin with, no really satisfactory vocabulary counts have been made of pre-school children's vocabulary. Those that do exist tend to be of the written language (e.g. of early essays), based on questionnaires about certain topics, or counts of the vocabulary used in children's books. This is not surprising. It is extremely difficult to obtain samples of spontaneous conversation from children, though recent advances using radio microphones are producing some promising results. In the meantime, there are many things teachers can do to obtain a more realistic sense of the child's vocabulary. One such idea involved the teacher 'following' the children from school to home, and noting the written language they were exposed to and which they seemed to take most notice of (e.g. in shop windows). This included such items as *Stop, Gentleman, High Street*, as well as *Drinka pinta milka day*, and a host of toy names and advertisements. There was literally no correspondence between this language and that adorning the walls of the classroom. Now it is a matter for discussion how much of this kind of language *should* be allowed in, but it is surely making non-sense of any principle of sociolinguistic expectancy to give it no place at all.

One of the main aims of the *Skylarks* programme, mentioned above, was in fact to try to bridge this gap between the conventional language of narrative function and that of the real world of diverse functions, by introducing such topics as road signs, warnings and instructions along with the statements and questions of everyday dialogue and monologue. But the point applies not only to grammar and vocabulary. It applies to the very basic concept of word and letter recognition. In a project entitled *ABC All Around*,[4] the aim was to make the principle of expectancy work for alphabet books. In this field, two factors are involved.

(a) The first is to ensure that the frequency of appearance of each letter reflects the relative frequency of appearance of that letter in the written language as a whole; and ensuring that the frequency of appearance of each letter initially, medially and finally in a word is reflected in the relative proportions of words given on the page. The following table illustrates the empirical facts which have to be taken into account: it is based on a count of all the letters occurring in initial, medial and final word position in all the items listed in several word counts of written vocabulary in children.[5] It is immediately apparent, for instance, that letters can be grouped into high, mid or low expectancy groups, simply on grounds of overall frequency (viz. high: *a, e, o, r, t*; low: *j, q, v, x, z*), and that certain positions within the word also carry specific expectations, as follows.

Most frequent	Second most frequent	Least frequent	
initial	medial	final	b, c, d, f, g, h m, p, s, t, w
medial	initial	final	a, l, o, u, z
medial	final	initial	e, n, r
final	medial	initial	k
final	initial	medial	y
initial	medial	(no final position)	j, q
medial	initial	(no final position)	i, v
final	medial	(no initial position)	x

It is easy to see, from such patterns, the impossible task a traditional alphabet book (of the 'A is for apple' type) sets itself ('X is for . . .?'), and how far removed from the letter-patterns of the real world it is.

(b) The second main factor is to reflect functional expectancy—ensuring that something of the enormous range of everyday differences in typeface, colour and style of lettering is represented, such as by showing words in signs, posters etc. as well as being merely labels for pictures.

[4] D. Crystal, *ABC all around* (in press).
[5] R. Edwards and V. Gibbon, *Words your children use* (London, Burke Books 1964); J. M. Wepman and W. Hass, *A spoken word count* (Chicago, Language Research Associates 1969); G. E. Burroughs, *A study of the vocabulary of young children* (Edinburgh, Oliver and Boyd 1957).

To do this successfully is no small technical linguistic (as well as artistic) task. How far it is a desirable innovation at child level remains to be seen (it is a widely used principle in adult literacy programmes, such as the *On the Move* series). It is however a logical consequence of accepting the general principle of expectancy, that the Bullock Report, amongst others, propounds.

Other proposals have been made to try to introduce some system into the provision of materials that are more realistic and appealing, both in the context of reading schemes and that of language development generally. The work of James and Gregory,[6] for instance, is an excellent way of introducing the powerful role of sound symbolism into the spoken and written language—of making children more aware of the potential in their voices, and of the effect of sound on reading. And such techniques as *Roll a story* or *Find a story* are of value not only in providing an appealing form of substitution drill that gives practice in using sentence patterns but also in drawing attention to the very notion of sentence, as an autonomous unit of meaning and structure.[7] As already pointed out in chapter 1, there is a considerable gap between the structural organization of colloquial speech and that of formal or written language: if the child is not used to hearing or responding to neatly organized stretches of language, the whole concept of 'organizing thinking' will need some systematic introduction.

The principle of appropriateness
The second principle focuses on the need for a systematic awareness of the extent and complexity of language variety. As argued above, language cannot be viewed as if it were a single, homogeneous entity, with a single set of forms and a single function. Language is a composite phenomenon, constituted by a range of dialects, styles and specialist uses, generally referred to under the heading of 'varieties'. The principle of appropriateness emerges out of this observation. The idea of appropriateness is now widely recognized in language-teaching contexts: the view that there is no single, universally correct or most logical use of language, and that acceptability depends primarily on seeing any language use in relation to its purpose—colloquial speech for informal situations, specialist terminology for scientific discussion, and so on. This 'democratic' account of language in use is seen in particular in those studies which have shown how the speech habits of children of different socioeconomic backgrounds vary—though whether these variations are sufficiently great to warrant calling them distinct 'codes' (as Bernstein does, for example) is highly debatable. An excellent discussion of the linguistic basis of this perspective as it applies to

---

[6] R. James and R. G. Gregory, *Imaginative speech and writing* (Nelson 1966).
[7] M. Vidler, *Find a story* (Penguin 1974), *Roll a story* (Penguin 1974).

regional and social dialects may be found in Peter Trudgill's *Accent, dialect and the school*.[8] Two questions clearly illustrate the force of the argument: the first is in a discussion of attitudes to accent in the context of the classroom:

> We conclude that children should not be asked to change or even modify their accents. Attempts to do this in school, whether through ridicule or more sympathetic methods, involve a serious danger of alienating the child from the teacher and the school, and are almost certain to fail because of the socio-psychological factors and other difficulties involved. If anyone, later in life, feels the need, for reasons of geographical or social mobility, to change their accent, they will be able to do this with a reasonable degree of success without formal instruction, simply through association with others who have the desired accents. This is a less conscious and, because of the continued reinforcement from others, much easier process than change in the classroom. (58)

The second quotation is from the corresponding discussion of dialect:

> Because of the relationship which exists between language and social class (and other sociological factors), language can be socially very symbolic. People therefore have attitudes towards different varieties of language which . . . in school . . . can be very important. Some children, for example, may find the teacher's language alien in some way, and come to resent the social gulf between them that the linguistic differences symbolise. Children may, usually in a subconscious fashion, find a teacher's dialect 'snobbish' or 'posh', and react to the teacher accordingly. There is little one can do about this linguistically. One simply has to reduce the gulf in other ways, and hope that a good relationship with the child will minimise the effects of his attitudes. Teachers should certainly not attempt to change their own grammatical forms or pronunciation towards those of the child. Unless the teacher is genuinely bi-dialectal, attempts to do this will usually be unsuccessful, and may be interpreted as insincere and insulting by the children. (60)

It is necessary to present these views at some length, in order to redress the balance from a time when the dominant thinking about language in education was to concentrate on the merits of the formal standard language at the expense of the various local dialects, accents and informal styles. It is also nececessary not to overstate the linguistic position. The attitude of linguists has sometimes been caricatured as a view that 'Anything goes' in language use, or that 'grammar doesn't matter.' Nothing could be further from the truth. The principle of appropriateness states simply that a use of language must be judged in its own context of use, and not by the standards of other uses which it was not intended to satisfy. It does not deny that there are standards— only that there are *absolute* standards. All varieties of English imply

8 P. Trudgill, *Accent, dialect and the school* (Edward Arnold 1975).

certain standards of usage to be judged as successful by other practitioners. Religious English naturally appears vague when judged by the standards of scientific language; but correspondingly, scientific English may seem pedestrian when judged by the standards of religious imaginative expression. Highly informal, colloquial language may seem out of place on the television news; but likewise, formal television news language would sound weird if used at the local club. Even informal conversation has its norms—if it is to remain successfully informal (see p. 24).

Comments such as that reported by Trudgill on page 61 of his book, therefore, have to be carefully interpreted, in their context, if they are not to mislead: 'As long as people are articulate, as long as they know what they're trying to say, it doesn't matter what sort of accent or dialect they use.' Such a statement applies literally only to regional and class varieties; it is not applicable to the study of the *stylistic* range of varieties that every dialect shows. We must by all means welcome expressiveness in children's use of spoken or written language, and encourage the use of those nonstandard forms that come naturally and powerfully to the child. On the other hand, spontaneous, informal expressiveness is not the only consideration, and the role of formal styles within dialects must not be minimized, especially in relation to the standard language. We have to be realistic. Whatever we think of the ideal of total dialect or stylistic tolerance, in all circumstances, it is at present and in the foreseeable future only an ideal. The children being taught now are going to have to grow up into a society where the formal standard language, in its various varieties, retains considerable prestige. Its practitioners still, in several walks of life, call the tune. And if the role of the teacher, at whatever level, is to prepare the child for normal participation in society, then he will be benefiting the child by providing him with as much command of the standard form of the language as is possible. And this will mean, inevitably, making him aware of the expected forms of language used in the various situations of formal 'educated' contact, along with the attitudes towards correctness that exist there. We may condemn such attitudes. We may wish to change society to remove some of the stigma that attaches to certain language forms. But it seems unreasonable to expect the child to do it for us, and unfair to give him the impression that 'anything goes, as long as it is sincere and expressive', when we know full well that in real life there are other linguistic standards that educated people are expected to live up to. It is not possible to change several hundred years of prescriptive sociolinguistic consciousness overnight. Particularly in the use of the more formal varieties of the written language, it matters; as Trudgill says on page 81, where he comments that 'most employers and managers will not look kindly on anything written in nonstandard dialect.' My point is that there are many careers where similar considerations apply to speech too, and it is therefore part of the task of the teacher to provide a groundwork of consciousness in the child which will permit him to anticipate the nature of the complex priorities that make up our linguistic world.

The current emphasis on language *in use* is a perfectly natural reaction against the older approach to language teaching, which involved parsing, clause analysis, and the learning of a seemingly endless set of grammatical terms. It is not my task here to go into the various justifications that were proposed for this approach (e.g. that it improved the child's speech or writing, that it was primarily a discipline for the mind, or that it was a basis for teaching foreign languages later), but it is important to stress the overriding weakness in the method—that language was presented as a 'dead' phenomenon. One took a sentence, analysed the parts, labelled them, and that was that. It was like a post mortem—but with the difference that what one was trying to discover was usually left obscure to the children performing the exercise. The analysis was seen as an end in itself, and it was unusual to see someone demonstrating a point in the exercise with reference to the living language. It *is* possible to make grammatical analysis live, but only if at all points we ask the question: what has been learned from the analysis of this sentence about the language as a whole? How far are the principles of our analysis powerful forces that we use many times a day to create new sentences, solve ambiguities, persuade, argue, joke...? Supplementing a formal analysis by an account of the *use* of linguistic structures immediately makes the exercise more promising.

But to move from formal parsing to considerations of use does not solve the problem: it simply sugars the pill. In practical terms, it is still a major and thankless pedagogic task if we have to work through a grammar book in class, getting terms and methods understood *before* going on to the 'interesting' part. For, apart from the problem of maintaining interest, there is the problem of not knowing in advance how much of the grammar-learning is going to be relevant, when we arrive at the study of uses. Thus the argument developed in the 1960s: would it not make greater sense to look at the uses of language first— at people's needs—and only then make a study of the features of language structure that are needed in order to fulfil those needs? This emphasis has been dominant recently, both in sociolinguistics and in linguistics. Approaches to linguistic analysis have become more semantically-oriented, with linguistics attempting to specify the *meanings* of utterances first, before incorporating information as to how these meanings are expressed in the syntax, lexis or phonology of the language. Sociolinguists have set up different kinds of classification of language uses, ranging from the broadest analyses in anthropological and ethnic terms to the minute analyses of behaviour in social psychological terms. And similar directions can be found in the various linguistic approaches to the study of literature.[9] In educational studies of language, the same emphasis has emerged, culminating in a number of projects where the aims have been to study the range of language uses that we might expect to be relevant to children at various stages of their education, and to provide materials which would enable the teacher to work with the child in exploring the function of language in the individual and in society. As the Bullock Report argued, 'the influence linguistics can exercise upon schools lies in [the] concept of the inseparability of language and the human situation' (174). The use of drama as a means of extending the child's consciousness of language has also been stressed, as has the collection and analysis of 'real-world' materials, whether on tape, video, or scrapbook. Reading schemes likewise have come gradually to reflect variations in use, though not usually in a very systematic way (see further below).

This functionalist perspective can be readily illustrated for all modalities of communication—speech, listening, reading and writing. To take the case of writing: the point is emphasized in the Schools Council project *Writing Across the Curriculum*, for example, where the distinctive function of writing (as opposed to speech) is stressed, and the various functions within writing discussed.[10] To see writing merely as a reflection of speech may have some justification in terms of formal structure, but is confusing as regards function. To see writing as an alternative to speech and no more obviously invites the question, 'Why bother to write, then, if I can speak?' (*Why write?* is the title of one of this group's publications.) It is presumably this confusion which underlies the query of the child who, having returned from a nature ramble and being told to 'write about it', asked, 'Why? It's easier to tell you.' What has not got across, from this response, it would seem, is the view that writing can do what speech cannot do, e.g. make thoughts permanent, precise, transmittable over distances, allow unique kinds of emphasis and variation (though the use of spacing, colour, size etc.). This view—and its corollary, that speech has a role that writing can never perform—*must* be got across, however, if awareness of *why* languages have varieties at all is to develop in children, and be the basis of more sensitive judgments and discriminations at a later age (such as those investigated by the Schools Council *Language in Use* project).[11] *How* such opinions might be inculcated in children I shall discuss below.

---

[9] For an account of semantic trends, see Palmer, *Semantics*. For sociolinguistic trends, see J. Gumperz and D. Hymes, *Directions in sociolinguistics* (Holt, Rinehart and Winston 1972). For stylistic trends, see Crystal and Davy, *Investigating English style* and Turner, *Stylistics*.

[10] N. Martin, P. D'Arcy, B. Newton and R. Parker, *Writing and learning across the curriculum 11-16* (London, Ward and Lock Educational 1976).

[11] P. Doughty, J. Pearce and G. Thornton, *Language in use* (Edward Arnold 1971).

The stylistic heterogeneity of the written language also receives emphasis in this approach. Here, one points to the happy coexistence in the adult language of styles of written communication that differ considerably in their formal features, because their functions are different. To see this, we need only compare an informal letter to a friend (with its relatively loose phrasing or punctuation—underlinings, dashes etc.) with a formal letter of application for a job. Situations where we feel the need to put forward our best side will also make us put on the linguistic habits that we think are 'best'. In educational discussion there has been a tendency to recognize three broad styles of writing: the purely personal, domestic style (as in letters, diaries, note-taking, logbooks); the 'creative writing' styles; and the 'business' styles, for such things as writing scientific reports. Each of these headings needs subclassification, of course, and there are some uses of language which seem to fall in between, but on the whole these general areas make a useful primary classification of written data. The analysis also carries a number of pedagogic implications, relating to the principle of stylistic appropriateness. Each variety has to be judged in its own terms. The standards for evaluating creative writing will not be the same as those for evaluating business writing. In this way, a compromise emerges between the two extreme positions concerning the correcting of written compositions: those who insist that all errors in spelling, grammar etc. must be corrected, and those who insist that expressiveness is all, and who do not correct. It is a false dichotomy, which assumes that all of writing has to be treated in the same way. There is a place for expressiveness, where we can judge the child's output in aesthetic and imaginative terms, and where we would not correct for its own sake because of the dangers of harming the child's spontaneity and confidence. On the other hand, there is a place for accuracy, convention and propriety, in those areas where it will be incumbent on the child to socialize, linguistically speaking—to integrate within a group, part of whose identity is the agreement to operate with a particular set of linguistic conventions (such as 'correct' spelling). It is doing the child no service to give him the impression that conventions do not matter—and of course the opposite also holds. In a real sense, the aim is to make the child a polyglot in his own speech and writing, by giving him a command of a *range* of formal patterns of language, the knowledge of when and where to use them, and the ability to put this knowledge into practice.

It is sometimes said, in opposition to this view, that this is surely making things too difficult for the child—that making him aware of language variety will only confuse him, whether in speech or writing. The answer to this is that it all depends on how the information about variety is introduced, in the classroom situation. 'Stylistic parsing' will of course confuse. But there are other ways of going about this. Let it not be forgotten, first of all, that the notion of appropriateness as such is not new to the average 5-year-old. As we have already seen (p. 55), from an early age children have come to be aware of the social uses of language. And particularly after they arrive in school, this stylistic consciousness increases enormously. The contrast between 'how we do it in school' and 'how we do it at home' becomes of major significance, to be shortly followed by 'classroom' versus 'playground' behaviour, and so on—all of which has a linguistic as well as a non-linguistic dimension. Seen in this light, the teacher who wants to develop a sensitivity to language variety has got plenty to work on. Of course, it requires a certain ingenuity to choose appropriate examples of language variety to work with, which do not go too far beyond the level of awareness of the child; but this can be the most enjoyable part of the whole exercise. I have observed a fascinating discussion amongst 6-year-olds of the notion of appropriateness, for example, which was introduced by making a taperecording of the *Magic Roundabout* programme, and playing the voices against the wrong pictures of the various animals. Once the laughter at showing Dylan with Dougal's voice had died away, it was relatively easy for the teacher to begin a discussion of why it was funny, and to generalize to types of voices in general. A drama element carried on the theme, as children were given various social roles which had clear, conventional linguistic markers (e.g. policeman, sergeant-major); and so on. It was evident that the children were developing their sense of style in the language, but doing so in a largely unconscious way. On the other hand, we must not underestimate the amount of preparatory work on the part of the teacher, who had to collect the stimulus material, select from it, and anticipate the follow-up work with some degree of precision. The same point could be illustrated from other styles of speech, such as the need for accuracy and precision in the giving of instructions. One technique that has been used here is the screen separating two children with identical sets of objects that have to be ordered into identical arrays. One child instructs the other and the results of the process are compared when the screen is removed.[12] And the way in which a sense of style may be developed can be illustrated also from the written language, where techniques that I have seen successfully used include confronting the child with a situation where the normal written cues have been removed (e.g. sending him shopping to a counter where the goods have no labels), or putting him in a situation where speech would be possible but not desirable (e.g. the passing of notes for secrecy). The possibilities are enormous.

It should be clear from these examples that in order for a functionalist approach to language teaching to succeed, we must be able to guarantee

---

[12] Cf. D. M. Gahagan and G. A. Gahagan, *Talk reform* (Routledge and Kegan Paul 1970).

the motivation of the children, by relating the kinds of language used to their real interests and backgrounds. This is the task of the teacher, not the linguist. But what the linguist can do is advise on the selection of material, on ways of simplifying it so that it does not lose its essential force, and on the identification of linguistic features that are likely to be new or intriguing to the children, of whatever age. From what has been said in chapter 2, for example, there will not be much point in using material that is full of linguistic ambiguities—puns, riddles, plays on words, etc.—much before age 7, and therefore the world of press advertising, which so often relies for its effect on such ambiguities (e.g. 'Our word is your bond'—advertising glue) ought to be used with great caution. The same point about motivation applies all the way up the age range. Indeed, after puberty, it seems to take on particular significance, in those situations where 'reluctance to learn' is endemic. There seems little point, for instance, in attempting to improve the spelling, grammar and so on of a class of 15-year-olds, if they have not been made to grasp the linguistic point of the exercise. Here, the view that 'my mates understand me, so what else do I need?' is common, and unassailable, unless we attack the situation at a more basic level. The first task is to establish an awareness of appropriateness as such, and this is itself often an extremely difficult thing to do. One teacher succeeded by getting a discussion going where the end was to elicit an admission from the class that they *did* care about the kind of language they used. He managed this not by contrasting their speech with the norms of the standard written language, but by breaking the class into boys v. girls, and comparing their slang, colloquialisms, and the like. It quickly emerged that there were 'girl-words', that the boys claimed they would never want to use (such as 'fabulous', 'divine'), and corresponding 'boy-words'. Another discussion focused on the difference between first-form language and their language. Once the differences had been recognized, it was easy to introduce the concept of appropriateness, which led to a discussion of the purpose of language, of degrees of success in using language, and ultimately to the role of the standard language and why it was worth while—economically, if for no other reason—to learn something of it. How long such motivation lasts with such groups, I do not know. There have been no studies. But such techniques at least provide the promise of progress, and are worth investigating further.

To develop the child's awareness of language functions, then, both receptively and productively, is a primary aim of any language policy. It is a pivotal issue, because it cuts across the traditional divisions imposed on language study—whether it is part of English only, or a foundation of the whole curriculum. A functionalist perspective caters for both views, by emphasizing the individuality of each function (in creativity, maths, science, religion . . .) without losing sight of the common core of structures that underlie them and make them all varieties of the 'one' language. It is sometimes useful, in fact, consciously to draw attention to the contrasts that distinguish these varieties, e.g. by introducing 'translation' exercises, whereby a text originally written for one purpose (e.g. scientific exposition) is rewritten as if it were part of an advertisement, part of a news story, and so on. It is even possible to focus on quite minute features of the different styles, e.g. moving from impersonal to personal as we go from science to magazine. But it is as we begin to consider the lengths to which we can go that certain limitations of the functionalist approach begin to emerge. The same limitations come to light if we are really trying to be systematic and comprehensive about the study of language use across the curriculum. For what *are* functions, in the final analysis? How many are there? How great *are* the differences between one function and the other? Is it possible to predict, from knowing someone's intentions, what kind of language he will actually use? In short, is the idea of language function capable of detailed and determinate specification?

The regrettable answer is that no one knows. No one has yet worked out a comprehensive classification of language varieties. Certainly, all the educationally-oriented projects have avoided this issue. They have chosen some of the most obvious and central functions to focus upon (e.g. the language of enquiry or persuasion), and it is the centrality of these ideas that has been their appeal. But no coherent theory of language functions in language development has yet been worked out, and if we look at the relevant areas of sociolinguistics or language acquisition, there is no sign of one. There are many promising ideas for the classification of speech functions (e.g. the distinction between 'expressive', 'poetic' and 'transactional'),[13] many insightful examples which show the nature of the problem, but little else. And as a result, much of the exposition of the study of functions in young children is vague and selective, concentrating on the clear cases, and skating over the many uses of language that seem to 'mix' language functions—where, for instance, it is difficult to classify a use of language as clearly expressive or clearly poetic. Such problems are well known in the literature on general or literary stylistics,[14] but they are largely ignored in the educational context.

Here are some examples of the theoretical difficulties. Does one talk of the 'variety' of advertising, or the 'varieties' of advertising? Is television and press advertising the same, or different, or 'basically' the same? Or is advertising as a whole no more than one subvariety of a grander variety of, say, 'propaganda'? Or again, to take the aim of

---

[13] See, for example, J. Britton, *Language and learning* (London, Allen Lane the Penguin Press 1971), 174 ff. Cf. also 74 above.
[14] See Crystal and Davy, *Investigating English style*, 60 ff.

'planned intervention in the child's language development' (Bullock Report, 67), an 'effective record' of language uses is given, corresponding largely to the set used in the Joan Tough project,

> Reporting on present and recalled experiences.
> Collaborating towards agreed ends.
> Projecting into the future; anticipating and predicting.
> Projecting and comparing possible alternatives.
> Perceiving causal and dependent relationships.
> Giving explanations of how and why things happen.
> Expressing and recognizing tentativeness.
> Dealing with problems in the imagination and seeing possible solutions.
> Creating experiences through the use of imagination.
> Justifying behaviour.
> Reflecting on feelings, their own and other people's.

But there is much selectivity and strange emphasis here. Why, for instance, is the language for 'expressing and recognizing tentativeness' singled out at the expense of such other social psychological functions as dominance or solidarity? And why are well-recognized functions of language, such as 'phatic communion' (viz. the use of language to promote a social atmosphere, as in casual chat about the weather) not listed at all? To sort out such questions demands a meticulous analysis of the similarities and differences between the different uses—most of which has not been done, at an academic level. To propound views about language functions in advance of the needed research is therefore hazardous, and it is not surprising that there is much confusion. Two teachers may both use a functional label, such as 'expository', about their pupils' work, but mean widely different things by it; and conversely, two quite different labels may be used to refer to more or less identical language.

Language functions and language forms

There is one way, and one way only, of avoiding the dangers of this situation, and that is by ensuring that those involved in introducing and assessing children's uses of language should be given a firm grounding in the principles that affect the nature of these activities. At least, we might argue, if we are aware of the theoretical and methodological difficulties inherent in the situation, we can be more cautious and self-critical about our procedures, and anticipate some of these problems. This I think is true. But to achieve this firm grounding takes a great deal more time and effort than some people seem to believe. The reason for this is that it is not possible to develop a systematic awareness of language functions without a corresponding awareness of the nature of language forms. If we do not balance these two dimensions of linguistic knowledge, there is no way to exert a measure of control on the theoretical position, and facts and hypotheses rapidly give way to opinions and feelings—supported, of course, by an appeal to 'experience'. The pendulum, which left formal grammar many years ago and moved in the direction of function, now needs to swing back some way—not to the 'post mortem' world of parsing, but to a position where the strengths of formal linguistic analysis are integrated within a functionalist perspective, and not ignored.

For they have been ignored, and in some circles the recommendation seems to be that they should continue to be ignored. The Bullock Report, for example, refers with favour to the view that formal knowledge of language is unnecessary: 'Is there anyone here who truly believes that it matters to anyone but a grammarian how you define a noun, or what the transformational rules are for forming the passive voice?' (174). The rhetoric is persuasive, with examples such as these, but it is irresponsible to suggest that the whole of formal language study is reducible to quibbling over definitions or the nature of transformational processes. The immediate point is that any polarization of function versus form is not only an unnecessary distortion of the nature of language, but the need for some kind of formal work on language is in fact unavoidable, if we want to make a functional approach work. Let us look at some of the arguments.

It should be clear from the above paragraphs that I fully accept the Bullock Report's view that the proper way to introduce systematic ideas about language is through the *use* of language. It would be difficult to find a linguist in this country who would advocate the resuscitation of traditional grammar-teaching in a modern (e.g. transformational) guise. I therefore agree with the four stages of language study introduced on page 162 of the Report:

(i) the learning of language comes from using and interrelating its different modes in various situations;
(ii) curiosity about language (e.g. about usage) may lead to ad hoc experiment and enquiry into the phenomenon;
(iii) systematic studies may then emerge, to develop the child's awareness of principles 'that may affect his understanding of himself and other people, rather than in any direct effect upon his language performance';
(iv) explicit rules may then be introduced, which will enable the child to solve particular problems or help him to re-analyse linguistic situations.

The trouble is, how are these principles to be put into practice by the teacher, in a conscious, controlled way? What knowledge must he have in order to implement these directives? The concepts of use and comprehension involved are very complex, susceptible to various interpretations, and give rise to major problems of assessment. As an example of the latter, given two children engaging in a 'use' of language, how are we to judge their relative success, or induce the less successful to improve? Apart from any pedagogic problems, the teacher must carry out at least four preliminary tasks:

(a) identify the difference between the two, i.e. determine which features of linguistic *form* account for their differing performance—for which he needs an awareness of language structure in general, a knowledge of some classificatory terminology, and a sense of the possible qualitative and quantitative variations affecting performance. He has to be able to answer the question '*How* different?'

(b) He must be clear as to the salient linguistic characteristics of a 'good' example of the language use being aimed for—assuming that it has been possible to isolate the notion of function in a meaningful way (cf. p. 77 above). What is a 'successful' instance of scientific, or persuasive, or instructional language, for example—and why is it successful?

(c) Once he has made a diagnosis, he must be aware of the possible linguistic pathways towards achieving this use of language which will affect decisions about teaching policy, e.g. whether he should build up a use of language in some graded, structured way.

(d) Having decided to implement a particular line of action, he needs to be able to identify progress—which amongst other things involves an ability to identify unexpected or misleading linguistic developments, such as the emergence of a structure which in fact militates against the development of the target use of language (e.g. the use of too many variations in pronoun or tense form in building up a style of scientific English).

In other words, the teacher must have some formal knowledge of language structure. And if he is not going to memorize examples of 'good' uses of language from every possible situation, which is hardly to be recommended, sooner or later he must learn some general rules about the nature of formal language variation, and the use made of this in social contexts, e.g. the types of pronunciation contrast expected in a given social context, or the limits of expected word order variation, or the restrictions on the generality of rules (e.g. how widely used *is* the passive in scientific English, and with which kinds of verbs?). Ultimately, this cannot be avoided, and the more systematically the teacher can be introduced to these problems the better. It simply will not do to imply that formal knowledge of language is unnecessary, or that it can be casually picked up as the days go by, or that there are no problems in applying the information.

The Bullock Report is of course only reflecting a view that has a fairly wide currency in the literature on language in the classroom, where an artificial opposition of language teaching and linguistics, the academic discipline, has emerged. This is the view that teachers do not need linguistics, but something which is referred to as 'language aware-ness' (or some similar phrase). This is said, for example, by the authors of the *Language in use* materials (a set of 110 units, each taking an aspect of language function, and suggesting strategies for classroom activity—cf. note 11 above): 'the teacher . . . is unlikely to find the central concern of the specialist in Linguistics, the explicit, formal and analytical description of the patterns of a language, immediately relevant to his needs' (11). Or again, in the first instance the teacher's job is 'not to impart a body of knowledge, but to work upon, develop, refine and clarify the knowledge and intuitions that his pupils already possess', and to study language functionally, pragmatically, 'the means by which individual human beings relate themselves to the world, to each other, and to the community of which they are members' (11). In a more recent publication the approach is developed into a philosophy of 'Language Study'.[15] What are the implications of these statements? On the face of it, they add up to a radical statement of dissociation. I think it is worth our looking at this point in some detail, as the implica-tions go well beyond the *Language in use* project as such, and raise issues equally applicable to any educational project which desires a linguistic orientation. I shall however restrict my illustration to *Language in use* in the first instance, having worked with the materials of this course at some length, and find that a great deal of value can be learned by looking carefully (and I hope constructively) at its limitations.

To begin with, it is worth pointing out that the view of linguistics found in the above quotations is very much a stereotype: it is a concep-tion of linguistics as a descriptive study, providing a detailed account of a language's structural properties, and so on. But this conception of linguistics is not fair to the subject *as it is taught* in universities in this country. The academic subject deals with both the formal study and the social, psychological and other implications. To treat linguistics as if it were an academic subject somehow separate from language in some social sense is to raise a straw man. *Language in use* is as much an exercise in linguistics (of one kind) as are practical exercises in phonetics (where people are taught to recognize and produce the range of possible speech sounds). The aims are similar, the presuppositions are similar—even some of the techniques are the same (e.g. some of the substitution exercises). Let us then be clear that we are talking about one kind of linguistics when we are examining the orientation of *Language in use*—at least this way we shall avoid having to talk about teachers 'languaging' pupils, and the like! My point is more or less recognized in Doughty and Thornton (see note 15 above), where a

[15] P. Doughty and G. Thornton, *Language study, the teacher and the learner* (Edward Arnold 1973), 47 ff.

distinction is drawn between a 'narrow' and a 'broad' view of linguistics: the former sees linguistics 'as a discipline which is concerned exclusively with the (organization of the sound patterns of natural languages, and their relationship to the corresponding organization of the internal pattern of those languages, phonological, grammatical and lexical' (49); the broad view sees linguistics as part of the study of human behaviour —the linguist J. R. Firth is quoted, the aim being 'to make statements of meaning so that we can see how we use language to live' (51). It is precisely a broad view of linguistics which I am insisting on. What I fail to see is the distinction between this and 'language study', in their sense—though perhaps this is not surprising, as it depends upon a highly abstract and ill-defined notion of 'agency' v. 'process' (see 51–2). But there are more important reasons for my attitude than this essentially terminological point.

The distinction between linguistics and language study is a good example of a pseudo-opposition, for the latter is dependent upon the former in certain crucial respects. Even if we accept the above restricted definition of the subject as a body of descriptive knowledge about structures—the 'narrow' view—it is possible to argue that this *cannot* be left out of the teacher's consideration, and that trying to do so causes more problems than it solves. *Language in use* claims that its aim is 'to provide an approach to the study of our own language that neither demands of the teacher specialized knowledge of Linguistic Science, nor requires of the pupil mastery of analytical procedures and unfamiliar technical terms' (8). This is defensible, for the pupil; but some such mastery is essential for the teacher, and indeed it is unavoidable. In the interests of consistency, coherence, and comparability, he needs some specialized knowledge and procedures. Without this information, he will find it impossible to achieve his aims. And much of the frustration felt by many teachers over the new emphasis in language study, I believe, is due to the fact that they fully see the point of the exercise, but having been led a little way along the road they are then left without any transport for getting to their destination, and moreover told that not only is transport not available, but that they should not even be thinking of asking for transport! Under such circumstances, no wonder many teachers decide not to travel.

The crux of the matter is that it is of course impossible to do without theoretical or descriptive terms in even the most casual analysis of language; and the argument continues that in that case they might as well be introduced systematically and used precisely. *Language in use* itself inevitably uses large numbers of such terms: intonation, noun, adjective, sentence, grammatical class, active voice. . . . Many of these terms are familiar, but of course their senses may be very different (e.g. the Hallidayan concept of 'transitivity'). And unless the teacher understands the basis and boundaries of this terminology, how can he carry out even the most elementary exercises involving it with confidence? For instance, a number of the units tell the pupils to go and look for other examples of the same kind of linguistic phenomena as the one being discussed. But how do we decide about what is same and what is different? That is the story of the whole history of linguistics, as the American linguist Bernard Bloch once said. And even within the units themselves, when the teacher is told to discuss how texts differ in syntax, or to work out some rules from a few sample sentences, what is this but explicit linguistic analysis? I frankly doubt whether many teachers could do this well without training. Either they would simply impose old-fashioned analysis on the sentences, which would rather miss the point of the exercise; or they would miss some of the differences between sentence structure; or they would set up oversimplified rules which would have to be quickly altered as new sentences were brought in by the pupils. The alternative, to print a typical set of sentences (which can be guaranteed to be analysed safely and regularly) would develop into the unthinking orthodoxy and inflexibility which it is the aim of the course to avoid. The only solution, it seems to me, is to learn enough linguistics to be able to anticipate and thus control these problems—but the time and practice it takes to develop the spontaneous awareness of linguistic identity, similarity and types of divergence is considerable. *Language in use* is wrong to minimize this problem. And so is the Bullock Report, when it says (175), 'It is, of course, up to the individual teacher to add to the assignments in each unit, or to omit from them what does not suit his purpose.' But my experience of discussing this point with teachers who have tried to do this is that it is precisely here that they find greatest difficulty, because they lack any formal training in how to extrapolate from the samples given, and how to evaluate what to reinforce or omit. The Report draws a comparison between studying 'specimens' of language and geographical or botanical field work; but where is the equivalent of the botanists' formal training here? *Language in use*, and other projects which work on similar lines, in effect takes teachers so far and then says 'Carry on': but one cannot, without specialist training, and the amount of this must not be underestimated.

Let us look at this from a different angle. *Language in use* provides many excellent ways of starting off a discussion, but it leaves the control of the ongoing discussion very much in the hands of the teacher—and this can lead to problems, without assistance. The teacher must know when to *stop* the discussion, having begun it—when to let it continue would involve the pupils in too complex issues; and this means he must be able to see thorny issues in advance, to see the possibilities in a line of argument, and so on. Three examples will illustrate this—one from phonology, one from semantics, and one from syntax.

In phonology, if accents are being discussed, and the difference between north and south of England emerges over the use of /a/, as in *bath*, the point will quickly be made that the north uses short /a/ whereas the south uses long /a/. But this is only partly true, as words like *hat* and *calm* indicate. The apparent exceptions can throw a teacher who does not expect them. Here, then, we have a tendency rather than a rule; and the problem for *Language in use* is that it regularly talks of rules, but not of tendencies. This is a general issue. Many of the questions *Language in use* raises do not have clear-cut answers, and the teacher must be prepared for this. This point is not sufficiently emphasized. For instance, in dealing with contrasts in intonation, voice quality etc., it is important to be aware that the pupils will not always produce agreed interpretations. In assessing 'distinctive voices', for example, as is done at one point, it is implied that the responses that will be obtained will be largely in agreement; but a teacher will be very lucky if this is so. Likewise, reactions to accent-interpretations will be extremely various, and some will be bound to be wrong. But will the teacher recognize differences in accents when he hears them, without some training? Or again, there are some rather basic phonetic 'facts' that would be invaluable material for a teacher—facts about language change or variations in acceptability. Statistical information could be obtained in project work, or the teacher could get it from various summaries of usage around. Either way, the study of English inevitably involves the imparting of some body of knowledge. I call this doing linguistics.

Similar examples could be given from other areas of linguistics. In the analysis of meaning (as in the unit on 'Birds and beasts'), the exercise is to list a set of objects and identifying features in the form of a grid, and then go through them indicating whether they are plus the feature or minus the feature. This is a good exercise, but the teacher ought also to know that there are many words in the language which do not work in this binary way. For instance, if the opposition 'liquid/ solid' is being used, then what is *tar* or *porridge*? And in syntax, the need to label word-classes consistently emerges; but questions such as 'Is *John* a noun?' or 'Is *asleep* an adverb?' can only be answered if the teacher is given some awareness of how parts of speech come to be established in the first place—the question of structural criteria again (cf. chapter 1). This inevitably involves some straight linguistic knowledge; but once obtained, the flexibility it gives the teacher is enormous. Once we know how terms come to be used, then we can tolerate differences between users, we can develop our own concepts, confident that we are not being self-contradictory, and so on—the methodological contribution, once again.

In short, while *Language in use* requires its pupils to make a largely ostensive analysis of language, accumulating inventories of features in texts they have collected for themselves, the teacher's job goes far beyond this, as he must be able to help them to generalize, to go beyond their texts, to get them thinking abstractly about what they are doing and what they can do. If the main aim of the exercise is to develop their command, or awareness, then it must be made clear that this will never happen as long as the pupils are restricted to exercises of the inventory type. Pointing out causes of particular functional effects is not developing a command; a command implies creativity, and to get this an awareness of the formal power of language is prerequisite. Instead of questions of the type 'What features were used in the text to obtain such-and-such an effect?' we need 'What other features could have been used?' Getting pupils to answer this last question is far more difficult, and requires fresh assumptions and techniques, which only linguistics can provide.

I have argued that pedagogic strategies for developing a fluent command of the mother tongue can succeed only if language awareness is underpinned on the part of the teacher by linguistics awareness. As already mentioned, this reasoning is applicable to far more than *Language in use*. The approach of Britton, Barnes and others also requires this underpinning. Their approach takes a general linguistic-educational-social hypothesis, and accumulates large samples of data as illustrative of the nature of the problem and of the ways available for attacking it. The authors' advice is effectively, 'Go thou and do likewise'. But how? The gap is still there, and it takes more than general books to fill it. For example, in a recent book,[16] the teacher is advised, rightly, not just to be aware and empirical, but to study language more systematically. But the authors then say, 'the relationship of language with learning should be an essential study. What this study might consist of is, of course, a matter for debate, but we suggest that perhaps a desirable course is not linguistics, psycholinguistics, or sociolinguistics, though these are important, but what we shall call educational linguistics'. Their outline which follows tells us only about the breadth of this study, however; there is nothing specific, and the teacher will surely be left wondering how the required systematicity is to be obtained if the only subject which can offer it to him, linguistics, is ruled out of court. The authors refer the reader to other books—Barnes *et al* (see note 18 below), Britton (see note 13 above) and Andrew Wilkinson's *The Foundations of language* (Oxford University Press 1971)—but even the latter, which is the most explicit about techniques, is a long way away from the kind of linguistic perspective discussed above.

I am wholly in favour of a functionalist perspective for linguistic studies, and I find the current emphases historically explicable: from a time when there was all formal analysis and no reference to function,

---

[16] L. Stratta, J. Dixon and A. Wilkinson, *Patterns of language* (London, Heinemann 1973), 140.

the pendulum has swung to the present approach. But the danger is to go to extremes, as a functionalist account of language with no formal controls can be just as sterile as the reverse. This, then, is where attention needs to be focused in the near future. Without some grounding in linguistic principles and procedures, the aims of the whole educational exercise in language work are unlikely to be achieved. The gap has got to be bridged, and it can only be, in my opinion, after a whole battery of syllabus studies have taken place. What *are* the linguistic constructs actually required by teachers operating at, say, sixth-form level? Could one work out the specific demands first, and then, as it were, write a grammar to fit? It remains to be seen. As it stands, at the moment, even if a teacher does become language aware, he is left in great doubt as to how he can assess his results, or compare them with others. Two teachers may differ radically about the new-found linguistic abilities of a child. In other words, attention now needs to be paid to evaluative procedures—to testing, criteria etc. This cannot be avoided. To take a final example, in the *Project on Writing Across the Curriculum*, there are many examples of children showing improvement after the recommended approach has been used. The interesting theoretical questions are why some children did not improve, or did not improve so much, or why teachers rate a particular kind of development more highly than others, or whether certain teachers get better results than others for a particular reason. Such questions cannot be answered as yet— indeed they are only beginning to be asked. Whatever the answers, it is quite clear that formal knowledge and systematic analytical techniques will play a large part in their formulation. But for the mother-tongue teacher, the question that should be being asked is not 'How little linguistics can we get away with?' but 'How much linguistics do we need?'

A unified approach?
The discussion so far has been based on two kinds of consideration: the nature of the practical linguistic problems encountered in teaching and therapy situations and the theoretical issues which such problems raise. My conclusion, after examining a whole range of such situations, in both classrooms and clinics, with adults and children, is that the similarities in the nature of these problems and principles are far more striking than the differences, and suggest the possibility of a unified approach to their study. Rather than have groups of primary teachers, speech therapists, remedial teachers and others studying these matters independently in their own conferences, journals and seminars, it would seem more satisfactory to mount a concerted attack, with teams of language specialists being brought to bear on the various issues which arise. At present, in view of the shortage of teachers and therapists, there is little time or opportunity to carry out systematic linguistic

analysis in relation to individual children; but if the general principles on which language work should be based can be worked out and agreed in an interdisciplinary context, this would by itself be a major breakthrough.

Such agreement on linguistic principles should not be an unreasonable thing to ask. Most of the issues raised in this book are equally applicable to 'normal', 'remedial' or 'therapeutic' teaching situations. The evaluation of what is a practicable teaching goal will differ from context to context, naturally, as will the techniques of interaction and remediation that stem from the particular training of the professional involved. But the same general kind of linguistic problems affect all contexts, and the same general methodological factors need to be borne in mind in attempting to solve them. I am thinking here not solely of those basic issues that arise as a matter of course in any discussion of educational principles—such as the importance of ensuring motivation as a prerequisite for learning, of planning of regular sessions, or of keeping systematic records of what has gone on. I am more concerned with the specific implications that arise from the focus on language as the topic of investigation. In particular, from chapter 2, it should be clear that *any* remedial work requires an awareness of the yardstick of normal development as a perspective for placing a child, assessing his progress, and as a means of suggesting fresh therapeutic exercises. In dealing with a child who is retarded in language development, it is by no means easy to judge the order in which we might present sounds or structures to him: knowledge of the facts of normal development both formal and functional (see chapter 2) provides one line on which to work. But precisely this knowledge, as we have seen, is essential in constructing or evaluating reading schemes or language development programmes. Across the field of language teaching, the need for a comprehensive account of the structures involved, graded in some way, to provide a clear and precise statement of teaching goals, is fundamental. Whether this is called 'screening', 'assessment', 'diagnosis' or whatever, is immaterial. The linguistic task is identical.

From chapter 1 it should also be clear that whatever the area of linguistic inquiry, it is axiomatic to try to live up to the standards of all scientific language work, and make our analyses as comprehensive, systematic, objective and precise as time permits. In the field of assessment and remediation in particular, it is crucial to adopt this perspective, if inaccurate diagnoses, wasted hours of therapy and mistaken educational placements are to be avoided. No one would accept partial, oversimplified and inaccurate evaluations in the more well-established professions, such as medicine or psychology. The surprising thing is that in language work such evaluations are common and uncriticized. I have already referred to the use of such measures as sentence length and part of speech counts as being too simple to be an accurate account of language structure (see p. 31): their use in assessment should therefore proceed with caution. Chapter 1 suggests the need to provide a systematic and complete account of language ability and disability. In practice, we are faced all the time with impressionistic portraits, which, while often correct as far as they go, are misleading in their selectivity. People take note of what strikes them, but this may be solely a function of the fact that a linguistic feature is more noticeable (e.g. an error in an irregular verb) or easier to talk about (e.g. the use of pronouns) or more familiar (e.g. the tense forms of the verb—but cf. p. 31). It is however the less noticeable features that are often more fundamental in any analysis, e.g. the pattern of word order, the way in which intonation is used, or the way in which sentences relate in meaning to each other—and these features are usually not so familiar, and require some mastery of new terminology. Above all, if our approach is not in principle systematic and comprehensive, there is an unavoidable danger of being misled by the nature of the sample of language selected for evaluation. It is always relatively easy to specify what is there, in a sample. It is far more difficult to specify what is *not* there, unless we have a general framework within which to 'place' the structures of the sample, to see how representative or consistent they are. A teacher or therapist engaged in the task of assessment needs to know not only where the child is, in terms of language development, but also where he is not. It is, after all, the absent structures that are the main focus of most remediation strategies.

The same point applies to the strategies themselves. Teachers and therapists need to know where *they* are, at any stage in the programme, and where they have got to go. A well-defined programme of immediate teaching goals needs to be laid down (geared, presumably, to some notion of normal development—see p. 62), and a *balanced* remediation or development programme established. The need to be in control of the programme at all stages is central. It is very easy, for example, to concentrate on a structure or use of language that a child is doing well in, to build upon it and extend it in various ways, and thus to achieve further progress. But caution is necessary, for in the process we can easily forget to deal with other, equally important structures or uses that the child needs to develop. By concentrating on one to the exclusion of others, we run the risk of developing an unbalanced linguistic skill, and of overestimating the child's linguistic ability. To avoid this, we have to make ourselves aware of the whole range of structures or uses that ought to be developing at a given stage; we must know clearly what we have not taught as well as what we have. It is sometimes difficult to *stop* working with language that has been successfully introduced to a child, and to turn to something else, but such decisions are crucial if a balanced linguistic skill is to emerge.

A similar point concerns the actual adult–child interactions. The adult has to be in control. Which means, for example, being able to anticipate the emergence of unexpected linguistic features in a session (e.g. the child produces commands when we were trying to elicit questions; a vivid idiom or metaphor instead of a mundane comparison; a back consonant or vowel in place of a front one), being able to recognize them for what they are, and decide whether to let them influence the immediate teaching, or to put them on one side for further attention. In one session with a language-delayed child, for instance, a therapist was attempting to develop a reasonably full clause structure, of a Subject–Verb–Object type. During one session, she found the child producing Subject–Verb–Adverbials, e.g. *The man ran quickly*, alongside *The man kicked the ball*. Being aware of the general structural similarities between these two sentences and knowing that they tend to appear at the same stage of development, she continued the session, reinforcing both, to good effect. (If that child had produced a passive voice structure, however, this would not have been reinforced at that point, as the development of passives is a much later skill (cf. p. 47).) There is always an element of risk in such situations: on the spur of the moment, we may make a decision we regret later. My point is that the more comprehensive, systematic and principled our teaching programme, the less risk there is likely to be.

Being in control also means pursuing a teaching goal despite the recalcitrance of the subject. It is particularly easy to be attracted by any answer that shows promise, and to seize on that as a basis for further interaction. With language work, however, this can lead to an anarchic situation, with the subject controlling (unconsciously or otherwise) the direction of the session, and making no linguistic progress. I have noticed this happening particularly when the teacher's structures make too many linguistic demands on the child: the child avoids the demands, and provides an alternative response, which is then accepted by the teacher. One 6-year-old child was recorded reading aloud to his toys at home in a flat, stilted, word-for-word manner, though his mother had often heard him read fluently to her. When asked why he was doing it, he replied that in school that was the correct way to read, for whenever he completed a sentence read thus, the teacher's comment was 'Very good!' More fundamentally, a speech therapist's attempt to elicit verbs from a child who previously had been using only nouns got into trouble when such questions were used as 'What's he doing?' 'What's happening in the picture?' Such questions *presuppose* verbs: to answer them, the child has to use a verb, which in this case he could not do, because of the nature of the disability. After several silences, the child pointed to the picture of a car and said 'wheels'. The therapist's reaction was one of praise—mixed with relief, perhaps, at having obtained a response at all. But linguistically speaking, the praise was in error. The child, after all, had produced the wrong answer to the question; he would make no progress if he always replaced a verb by a noun. By accepting the response, the therapist had effectively lost control of the session at that point. (She might have regained control, of course, by *paraphrasing* the child's response, with appropriate emphasis on the verb, e.g. *Yes the car's got wheels, and the man's driving the car, isn't he?* Alternatively, she could avoid using such questions altogether, until such time as the child is more ready for them.)

These examples relate to questions of both assessment and remediation; but in the last analysis, these two areas cannot be divorced. One of the main problems with language-teaching materials at present is that they do one thing but not the other: they assess, but they do not teach, or vice versa. Yet surely any language programme ought to be capable of relating to both: of saying where a child is in terms of language development, and at the same time saying where he ought to be, and making suggestions as to how to get him there. In my opinion, only approaches linked to language development scales and comprehensive linguistic analyses (whether of sounds, grammar or meanings) stand a change of doing this. But even these have certain limitations in the present state of knowledge. In particular:

(a) There are so many variables involved that it is not feasible to think in terms of a single 'score' for pronunciation, syntax or whatever. A number of scores are widely used, but they have to be interpreted with caution, for two individuals could achieve identical scores for totally different reasons. Nor do scores help in answering the question 'What linguistic feature to teach next?'. Profiles, however, do. A profile is a qualitative display of the range of linguistic features present, statistically analysed in some way. From it, we can see the areas of strength and weakness, and also possible paths of development. Part of the syntax profile chart from *The grammatical analysis of language disability* is reproduced below. Even without knowing exactly what the labels stand for, it is obvious that here is a child who is (a) delayed and (b) unbalanced in his syntactic skills. If he is 4½ years old, a half-hour sample should provide well over 100 sentences, whose complexity would be shown by a scatter of figures down the chart as far as Stage VI (the Stages correspond to those outlined in chapter 2, page 45 ff.). In fact he produced relatively few sentences, apart from 'social' monosyllables such as 'yes' and 'no': and those he did produce group in a skewed distribution around Stages I, II and III. He has several structures at phrase level (e.g. *nice hat*—Adjective + Noun), but only one at clause level; verbs in particular are conspicuous by their absence, and as a result the fully developed range of clause types is lacking (e.g. *Daddy kicked the ball*—Subject + Verb + Object); he uses statements but no questions, commands or exclamatory structures, and is generally

Stage		Minor **39**			Social **35**	Stereotypes **4**	Problems		
Stage I (0;9–1;6)	Sentence Type	Major **56**				Sentence Structure			
		Excl.	Comm.	Quest.			Statement		
			·V·	·Q·	·V· **1** ·N· **16**	Other **12**	Problems		

Stage			Conn.	Clause			Phrase		Word
Stage II (1;6–2;0)		VX	QX		SV	V C/O	DN **5**	VV	**1** -ing
					S C/O **2**	AX	Adj N **3**	V part	**4** pl
					Neg X	Other	NN **7**	Int X	
							PrN **1**	Other **8**	-ed
Stage III (2;0–2;6)		VXY	QXY		X + S:NP	X + V:VP	X + C/O:NP **2**	X + A:AP	-en
		let XY	VS		SVC/O	VC/OA	D Adj N **1**	Cop	3s
		do XY			SVA	VO_dO_i	Adj Adj N **2**	Aux	
					Neg XY	Other	Pr DN **2**	Pron **1**	gen
							N Adj N	Other	
Stage IV (2;6–3;0)		? S	QVS		XY + S:NP	XY + V:VP	XY + C/O:NP	XY + A:AP	n't
			QXYZ		SVC/OA	AAXY	N Pr NP	Neg V	'cop
					SVO_dO_i	Other	Pr D Adj N	Neg X	'aux
							cX	2 Aux	
							XcX **1**	Other	
Stage V (3;0–3;6)		how	tag	*and*	Coord. **1**	**1** ·	Postmod. **1** clause	**1** ·	-est
				c	Subord. **1**	**1** ·			-er
				s	Clause: S		Postmod. **1** · phrase		
		what		Other	Clause: C/O				-ly
					Comparative				

	(+)			(−)				
	NP	VP	Clause	NP		VP	Clause	
Stage VI (3;6–4;6)	Initiator	Complex	Passive	Pron	Adj seq	Modal	Concord	
	Coord		Complement	Det	N irreg	Tense	A position	
						V irreg	W order	
	Other			Other				

Stage	Discourse			Syntactic Comprehension	
Stage VII (4;6+)	A Connectivity	*it*			
	Comment Clause	*there*		Style	
	Emphatic Order	Other			

Total No. Sentences **95**	Mean No. Sentences Per Turn	Mean Sentence Length

Figure 5 Section from syntax profile chart: Peter F, age 4;6

weak in spontaneous language use. Similar profiles could be developed for other areas of language, as soon as enough empirical information is available.

(b) At present, the differences between individuals are as striking as the similarities. It is extremely difficult to group children or adults into language-ability groups in anything other than the grossest terms. Classification (or diagnosis) is premature. As a consequence, the most satisfactory teaching or therapy at present proceeds along individual lines, i.e. progress in the individual is the aim, without insisting on the need to 'type' him.

(c) One needs to be trained to evaluate language-development procedures. Much has been said in this book of the 'scientific' nature of linguistics. But it would be irresponsible to suggest that the canons of scientific rigour aimed at by linguists have been achieved in all areas of the subject. On the contrary, there are many topics which have either received no study at all, or where there is only speculation, supported by few or no facts. I believe that in such a field as child-language studies, enough basic information has been accumulated to make the construction of developmental scales feasible and useful—and this belief will be judged by its results. But it must be emphasized that developmental charts, totals, and other descriptions are only one small part of the linguist's aim in this matter—to arrive at an overall explanation of the child's developing ability—or even to characterize the notion of 'ability' itself. And there is much controversy as to how and how far such aims can be achieved. In other words, there is no substitute for the teacher or therapist learning enough about the background of ideas in child language and linguistic studies to be able to evaluate the concrete proposals about assessment and remediation which are emerging. Only in this way can we avoid the temptation of seeing a new technique or scheme as fixed and uncriticizable. Once we have learned to master a new technique (knowledge 1), we need to learn its strengths and limitations, its applicability to our own situation and how to modify it (knowledge 2). So far, in discussing the use of language techniques, most of the concern has been with knowledge 1—about the unfamiliarity of terms, symbols, and so on. But this is the tip of the iceberg. It is knowledge 2 which is the real goal.

(d) Just as we must not underestimate the amount of knowledge it takes to implement a systematic language-teaching procedure, so we must not underestimate the question of time. There is always a tension between the demands of accuracy and comprehensiveness of analysis, on the one hand, and speed and simplicity of use on the other. It is up to the teacher or therapist to judge how best to arrive at the optimum balance between time spent on matters of analysis and interpretation, and time spent in actual therapy or teaching. But the hard fact of the matter is that most aspects of language structure and use require time, if their secrets are to be revealed. It simply is not possible to analyse the pronunciation, grammar or semantics of a sample without being prepared to spend time on it—perhaps 2 hours for the pronunciation of a 15-minute sample, 3 or more for its syntax. The question is, Is it worth it? Everyone professionally involved has to decide this for himself—so the facts must be stated plainly. And so must the implications. If we cut down on time for analysis, what do we lose? It is my view that simple analyses of complex phenomena only postpone problems; they do not solve them, and they may obscure them. If we want to analyse language properly, therefore, an outlay of time must be anticipated. If we are not prepared or able to spend this time, then this is regrettable—but we must then be realistic, and not claim that we have 'carried out a language assessment', when all that has happened is 30 minutes worth of selective thumbnail sketching.

But the problem of time must be set in perspective, and assessed over the *long term*, in relation to the total anticipated contact time between adult and subject. The argument here is that time spent in analysis and interpretation in the *early* stages of teaching or therapy is likely to save time later on, and obtain more definite progress in the meantime. The responsibility is to the individual child or adult, patient or pupil. The question 'Can I afford the time to do it?' really has to be reversed: 'Can I afford not to do it?'

It must be admitted, however, that there is no real solution to the time problem until more realistic job-assessments take place, in which the central role of teacher and of therapist as language evaluator is recognized, and time and assistance made available to carry out the task. It is possible, for example, that the new concept of speech therapists' *aides* might be fruitfully used to cut down on the labour of linguistic analysis—at least for its more mechanical aspects. Another suggestion is that special language-analysis centres be established, in which the task of detailed analysis of samples of usage would be carried out—in much the same way as the pathology laboratory serves a hospital. Or, of course, one could increase the number of teachers, therapists, and others. There are many possibilities. All need money, and realistic awareness at national level of the size of the problem. There is no sign of either, at the moment.

Given the practical difficulties, it is hard to see at present how such recommendations as Bullock's can be implemented:

> If the success of remedial measures is to be broad and lasting, a recognition of certain factors is essential: (*i*) the *particular* nature of *each* child's difficulties must be seen in relation to his *whole* linguistic development. . . . (219)

> The outcome of the observation procedure [in screening] should be a *detailed* profile of each child's strengths and weaknesses. (198) (my italics)

Both in terms of time for training and time for carrying out screening, the size of the linguistic task has been seriously underestimated. But at least, after many years, the nature of the problem has begun to be precisely identified. And it is not the case that nothing can be done. There is in fact a great deal of practical value that can come from a general discussion of the principles involved.

A typical example of the immediate pedagogic consequences of a general principle comes from a series of group discussions held for the staff of a special school. The principle being advocated was the need to make the linguistic environment of the child *consistent*. Some degree of consistency in sound, vocabulary and structure is essential in any teaching context. It is crucial in remedial work where one factor in the disability is likely to be a difficulty in assimilating and integrating linguistic variability—whether due to limitations on perception, memory, attention, or other reasons. 'Flooding' the child with language may sometimes help, but it can often hinder, and it goes against the need for a principled therapy, because we have no control over the input. The need to plan the environment explicitly, and provide a programme of language development that *all* concerned with the child can follow is essential. But it is difficult to implement. In one special school, for example, in one hour a child's favourite toy was variously referred to as 'teddy' (by his teacher), 'ted' (by the educational psychologist), 'bubu' (by the nursery assistant), and 'Freddy' (by his parent). If this kind of variability is going to be at all widespread, then it will not be surprising that development will be slow. Normal children seem to have a remarkable ability to cope with such variations; but not remedial children. What is needed in such circumstances is an explicit account of the language that the team agrees should be used to the child (as well as of that which he himself uses). Wall-charts, diaries, tapes, or other displays are means of doing this. Nor is it ever too early to begin this process—though the earlier one starts, the more a certain degree of phonetic skill is required to map variations in the vocalizations with a reasonable degree of precision. The importance, also, of keeping the adults' intonation fairly stable ought not to be underestimated. For children (or adults) at the early stages of language development, the intonation, rhythm and general 'tone of voice' of speech is the major perceptual factor. They respond to this long before they do to the segmental or verbal side of speech (see p. 38). To alter radically the intonation of a sentence may then be equivalent to hearing a whole new sentence, to the disordered person. A good example was in a drill where sentences like 'That's a cow' were being presented for imitation to a patient. Each time the patient imitated successfully. However, when the therapist switched to 'That's a big cow', with the emphasis on the adjective, the patient responded immediately by following the intonation, and produced 'That's a big'. Despite the fact that her auditory memory was good enough to cope with the longer utterance, she none the less stopped the sentence at that point, as the rhythm of the previous sentences had led her to expect to do.

A second example of the kind of practical applications that stem from general principles arose in considering the need for the adult language to suit the *level* of the child or patient. This principle has both a formal and a functional application. From the formal point of view, it would mean choosing a style of language compatible with that of the child—more specifically, choosing vocabulary within his comprehension range, sounds that he is capable of discriminating, and structures that are within his analytical abilities, as far as we can tell. Presumably, any of the 'later' structures outlined in chapter 2 would be problematic for the average 5-year-old, for example. But at times, the issue may be more fundamental: a case in point is the difficulty some children have in responding to questions, the answers to which are already known to the questioner (i.e. the normal teaching strategy). They may respond with silence or irrelevance, not because they are stupid or antipathetic, but because they have had little experience in their home backgrounds of being questioned in that kind of way. They may not 'see the point' of the question, or lack a command of the appropriate response patterns.[17]

This principle also means reacting to the child's language in appropriate ways. Based on what is known about mothers' responses to child speech, various strategies suggest themselves, e.g. the need to expand and paraphrase responses (cf. p. 56), the need to check that comprehension of a word or structure is there before expecting a child to use it constructively in production, or the need to check that the assumptions the teacher is making are shared by the child (cf. p. 57). A good example of this *not* happening is given by Douglas Barnes.[18] He quotes the following extract from a recorded dialogue between teacher and secondary school pupil concerning life in New Testament Palestine:

T   How did they get the water from the well? . . . Do you remember? . . . Yes?

[17] W. P. Robinson and S. J. Rackstraw, *A question of answers* (Routledge and Kegan Paul 1972).
[18] D. Barnes, 'Language in the secondary classroom', in D. Barnes, J. Britton and H. Rosen, *Language, the learner, and the school* (Penguin 1969), 33–4. For further discussion of the language of pupil–teacher interaction, see J. J. Gumperz and E. Herasimchuk, 'The conversational analysis of social meaning', in R. Shuy (ed.), *23rd Annual Round Table* (Georgetown 1972), 99–134; J. McH. Sinclair and R. M. Coulthard, *Towards an analysis of discourse* (Oxford University Press 1974).

P1	They . . . ran the bucket down . . . er . . . and it was fastened on to this bit of string and it . . . (here the words become inaudible for a phrase or two) . . . other end to the water.
T	You might do it that way . . . Where did they put the water . . . John?
P2	In a big . . . er . . . pitcher.
T	Good . . . in a pitcher . . . which they carried on their . . .?
P2	Heads.

Barnes points out that the first answer is a perfectly appropriate response to the open question asked, but is met with a negative reply—'You might do it that way', in fact spoken by T with a doubtful intonation. He goes on:

> Pupil 2 suggests an answer *of a different kind*; he intuits—or remembers—that his teacher does not want improvised reasoning but the name of an object. His reply . . . is accepted and carried further with a promptness which signals *to both pupils* that this is what was required in the first place. It might be surmised that these pupils are not only learning about Palestine but also about the kinds of reciprocal behaviour appropriate to a teacher–pupil relationship, that is, learning when not to think.

There are many other relevant general principles. The principle of *systems* of linguistic contrasts immediately raises questions of how to introduce items such as prepositions, articles and conjunctions: the way in which definite and indefinite articles define each other, for instance, suggests the need to devise ways of teaching them so that the contrast in their use is made explicit, and not left to be 'picked up by association', as happens when they are taught in isolation from each other. The principle of motivating the learner by introducing familiar and appealing language raises evaluative questions of a basic kind: teachers and therapists need to acquire something of the psychological insight of the children's author, who tries to see the world from the child's point of view. The point is in no way restricted to young children, however: it applies equally to the adolescent and to the disabled or disadvantaged adult. Unfortunately, relatively little progress has been made in seeing the linguistic potential in material such as disc-jockey commentaries, jokes, television dialogues, and the like. In the case of one adult aphasic, for example, a marked improvement in positive behaviour emerged when the therapist switched from a routine session using pictures of objects, animals etc., to one where they went into the objects and events that surrounded horse-racing, the patient's favourite sport. A similar case concerned a group of 10-year-olds in a special school, whose language was characterized primarily by inability to organize sentences into coherent dialogues or speech 'paragraphs'. A systematic concentration on the use of coordinating and subordinating conjunctions was not working very well, until the idea was proposed to turn the exercise into a game (something like 'Consequences'), where the children took turns to build up a story, but were given the various grammatical items to introduce their own contribution. There are many kinds of drill, involving substitutions, transformations and other things, that can be modified for use as games with children. The literature on foreign-language teaching is an excellent place to start accumulating ideas along these lines.[19]

Above all, there are many language-learning myths that can be readily exploded, with relatively little technical knowledge, thus leaving the ground clear for positive and constructive thinking. Examples would be the view that there is no system in English spelling, or that children babble sounds from all the world's languages: both views are wrong, though it requires a certain amount of study before this can be demonstrated.[20] Here is an example in more detail—the view that the children of bilingual parents will be linguistically disadvantaged. Once again, the linguistic contribution is not necessarily to provide an answer: it is to make people aware that there is an issue. The 'commonsense' basis for this view of bilingualism is presumably that a child exposed to more than one language will be likely to confuse them; and his development of either language will accordingly be slower and poorer. As very few systematic studies of bilingual language acquisition have been carried out, it is not possible to produce a critique of this reasoning on empirical grounds. Evidence on both sides is anecdotal: one person will cite a case that led to problems; another will cite one where there was no trouble at all. But on theoretical grounds, there are some salient points.

What is meant by the term 'bilingual' is by no means self-evident, to begin with. A situation where a child is exposed to two languages from birth in absolutely equal proportions is highly improbable. The language of one parent (usually the mother) will be overwhelmingly in the majority for the first two years or more. Also, general studies of adult bilingualism have shown that it is uncommon for two languages in a bilingual situation to be genuine alternatives: usually, one language relates to one social role (e.g. formal or professional interchange), the other to a different role. The languages do not get mixed up as long as the social settings which give rise to them remain clear. We might then conceive of a similar situation with the young child, where 'father-talk'

[19] See, for example, the periodical *English Language Teaching* (Oxford University Press) or the introduction by W. F. Mackey, *Language teaching analysis* (Longman 1965).

[20] On spelling, see L. A. Hill and J. M. Ure, *English sounds and spelling* (Oxford University Press 1963); W. Haas, *Phono-graphic translation* (Manchester University Press 1970). On babbling, see 39 above, and also D. K. Oller, L. A. Wieman, W. J. Doyle and C. Ross, 'Infant babbling and speech', *Journal of Child Language* 3 (1976), 1–11.

and 'mother-talk' will be clearly differentiated. He talks in one way to mother; in another way to father. This happens to a certain extent even within a language: by the end of the first year, the child has encountered many styles of speech directed to him (e.g. baby-talk, lullaby, 'man-to-man'), and his own 'talk' has been affected: his pitch level varies depending on whom he is 'talking' to (higher to the mother), role-play features begin to emerge in his babble, and there are clear signs of stylistic differentiation.[21] We might then argue that this is no different in principle from the situation of a child encountering two languages, rather than two varieties of the same language. After all, the *child* does not know that they are distinct languages. In short, there is no theoretical reason why a bilingual situation should necessarily pose the child with extra language learning problems over the first few years. If the language environment is natural, consistent and stimulating, the child will pick up whatever languages are around—and a considerable proportion of the world's children are in fact reared in a multilingual setting. On the other hand, if artifice is introduced into the environment, e.g. by trying to maintain a 'balanced' exposure to the two languages, or by introducing a bias towards one language, say, for political reasons, then it is likely that the adults will begin to be inconsistent, the clear social roles of the languages will blur, and linguistic confusion leading to delay may result, perhaps with associated behaviour problems. I emphasize again that the issue is incapable of scientific resolution at present. But no resolution will come until the existence of the problem is recognized and the myth of inevitable deterioration dispelled.

These issues cross-cut the various teaching and remedial disciplines, and once more suggest the importance of a unified approach to their study. But in seeking such an approach, one category of person must not be forgotten: the parent. And with parents must be grouped the whole range of relatives with whom subjects are in regular contact, as well as the 'ancillary' staff in institutions. Taken altogether, these people provide what is often the bulk of the language directed to the child or adult. Seen against their potential contribution, the role of the teacher in a large class, or a therapist with a large case-load spread over a wide area, is put in perspective. It is important not to underestimate this, as the remarkable progress in the aphasia of Patricia Neal showed.[22] If language problems are involved, it seems unlikely that any remedial procedure would succeed if direct intervention by the professional is limited to a matter of minutes per day or a half-hour

[21] See L. Kaplan, 'Speech registers in young children', *Child Development* **44** (1973), and Crystal, *The English tone of voice.*
[22] V. Eaton Griffiths, *A stroke in the family* (Penguin 1970).

per month—as so often happens. Until such time as class sizes and case-loads become manageable, therefore, teacher and therapist must rely on the reinforcement of these others. At the very least, they must ensure that there is no contradiction between home and school, or home and clinic.

But how is such cooperation to be achieved? For parent–professional cooperation to be successful, certain conditions need to be present, of which mutual knowledge and good communications are prerequisite. The professional must *know* the home linguistic background if he is to devise a teaching strategy that matches it—and this involves decisions at both individual and local authority level, e.g. inviting a parent into class or clinic, or arranging for reception-class teachers to visit the pre-schoolers at home, (as is done in some areas). The parent, likewise, needs to *know* the aims and assumptions of those engaged in teaching the child, if there is to be fruitful collaboration. To an extent, therefore, the professional has to 'teach' the parents about language—or at least, inform them about the kinds of ways in which they can help. There are now an increasing number of materials available to provide a basis for this, e.g. the pamphlets produced by the College of Speech Therapists,[23] or the forum provided by associations such as the United Kingdom Reading Association (UKRA) or the Association for All Speech Impaired Children (AFASIC).[24] And there is a great need for information and guidance, in view of the popular myths and misconceptions about language development which abound. Some specific examples of advice that I have observed to be particularly germane have included: the importance of maintaining a good flow of talk directed to the young child, especially in contexts where one might find it easier to leave well alone, e.g. at bathtime; the need to link language with purposeful action wherever possible (cf. p. 56); the need to avoid talking *for* the child, not giving him enough time to work out a reply for himself; the need to be aware of normal or expected 'errors', such as the hesitant fluency of the 2-3-year-old (sometimes mistaken for stammering), or the immature grammar of the early stages; correspondingly, the importance of avoiding explicit correction (cf. the 'indirect' correction illustrated on p. 90), and the various ways of expanding and reinforcing normal speech patterns; and so on. In addition to these general ideas, it is also often possible to involve the parent in specific language-teaching strategies, as long as the importance of flexibility is emphasized (i.e. not sticking to a drill pattern too rigidly or mechanically). An example of this possibility is given on pages 64–5 above.

[23] 'Teaching your child to talk', 'Are you worried about your child's speech?' and other pamphlets may be purchased from the College of Speech Therapists, 47 St John's Wood High Street, London NW8 7NJ.

[24] AFASIC, Toynbee Hall, 28 Commercial Street, London E1 6LS.

It is impossible to say, at present, how far the whole of linguistic training, assessment and remediation can be put on a confident, systematic basis. The field is still in its infancy. Over the next decade, a great deal will come from the many projects involved in providing materials aimed at filling some of the needs described in this chapter. But there is no room for complacency, even now. No matter how well constructed language materials are, they are useless in the hands of someone who lacks the knowledge to use them. And this means far more than knowing how to put them into practice in a classroom: it means appreciating the principles on which they were based, being able to see their strengths and limitations, and having the confidence to modify them to suit one's own teaching situation. All of which depends on mastering some sort of groundwork of linguistic ideas and strategies—a process which will take time and which therefore, needs to be begun at the earliest opportunity. Nor is there room for premature pessimism. The 'they'll learn anyway, so why bother' argument is unfortunately all too often heard. '*I* learned to read (etc.), so why do we need all these new fangled ideas?' Such arguments are indefensible theoretically, pragmatically and even, at times, ethically (particularly with language disorders, where the variables are so complex that only systematic approaches stand a chance of giving treatment a coherent explanatory basis). It is true that the older methods usually 'worked', but why they worked is unclear (e.g. the role of a gifted teacher, of punishment, of a world without television), and how well they worked will never be known. Who knows what problems were caused by the use of the early reading schemes? The merit of the newer approaches is not that they will *necessarily* teach language skills better, but that they are *explicitly principled*: the user is more in control, more able to predict strengths, and problems, and develop a coherent explanation of what he is doing. There is, this way, more chance of achieving an intellectually satisfying and confident understanding of one's professional competence. And it is on this basis that my arguments for using the findings and principles of linguistics stand.

Author index

Subject index